PHOTOGRAPHY BY
SØLVI DOS SANTOS

TEXT BY
LANNING ALDRICH

MAJORCA

IBIZA, MENORCA, AND FORMENTERA

STEWART, TABORI & CHANG

NEW YORK

CONTENTS

The Balearic Islands are easily overlooked on a European map – you may have to spend a little time searching for them. Yet these small islands share an impressively strong identity, and each one can also claim a distinctive character of its own. This is due as much to the islanders themselves as to the great number of immigrants from the Spanish mainland and all over the world. In general, those who have chosen to live here are not Robinson Crusoes who have just drifted ashore by accident. Mostly they are well-traveled, cosmopolitan people who have consciously decided to set down their suitcases and create their own private paradise.

This was confirmed for me when I headed back to Ibiza two years ago, having not been there for more than twenty years. My friend Bruno Reymond, who had successfully switched from "gray Paris to the sunny islands," invited me to stay and managed to convince me that here, there was enough rich material for a book. He was right. The owners of the houses in this book, many of whom have dared to break away from lives elsewhere, are a fascinating group. They seem to feel free to live out their fantasies through their homes, whether they have restored an old building, had a new house designed, or even built one with their own hands. These very personal homes freely mix possessions gathered from many far-flung places: furniture bought on trips to Asia, India, Cuba, or North Africa; local crafts and antiques; and ethnic items from the local hippie markets. As the end product of many style decisions, these homes reveal much about their owners' true nature. Often their beauty results more from an abundance of creative energy than a huge amount of money.

Finally, please note that the pictures in this book reflect real-life situations; I have certainly not attempted to improve upon reality by using stylists or larger-than-life flower compositions. I'm very grateful to have been able to both photograph and enjoy these "private worlds."

For many generations the Balearic Islands have been a popular destination for those in pursuit of summer and winter sunshine; but for just as long, these lovely Mediterranean islands have attracted people seeking artistic inspiration. This book shows some of the more unusual and creative homes in the islands – ranging from a converted shepherd's shelter to the ultimate in contemporary architecture. What these houses share is an affinity for the spirit of the place; imagination, flair, style, and humor are combined to create dwellings filled with the personality of their owners.

The four islands also possess personalities of their own; although the Balearic Islands form an archipelago extending from the Spanish mainland, in topography, each island differs substantially from the others. Majorca, the largest of them, has a wide variety of landscapes within its area of roughly 1,400 square miles, with a rugged mountain range – the Serra de Tramuntana – running the length of the northwestern coast and its highest peak – Puig Major – rising to 4,740 feet. Another less dramatic range, the Serra de Llevant, is on the southeastern coast, while in the center of the island, a fertile agricultural plain stretches toward the southwestern shore with its gentle, sandy beaches. Menorca's topography is more subdued: low, fertile hills and valleys in the north and an arid limestone plain to the south, with accessible coves and beaches shaping its coastline. Ibiza consists of pine-clad hills throughout the island, with a coastline of rugged stone cliffs interspersed by sandy coves. Formentera, the smallest of the Balearics, is covered with low scrub in its center, with gentle hills at one end, dramatic rocky cliffs at the other, and a flat, sandy strip of beach in between.

Situated as they are midway between Spain and North Africa, the Balearics have always provided a natural stopping-off place for all sorts of travelers: seafarers on their way to and from the Atlantic Ocean, merchant traders engaged in all

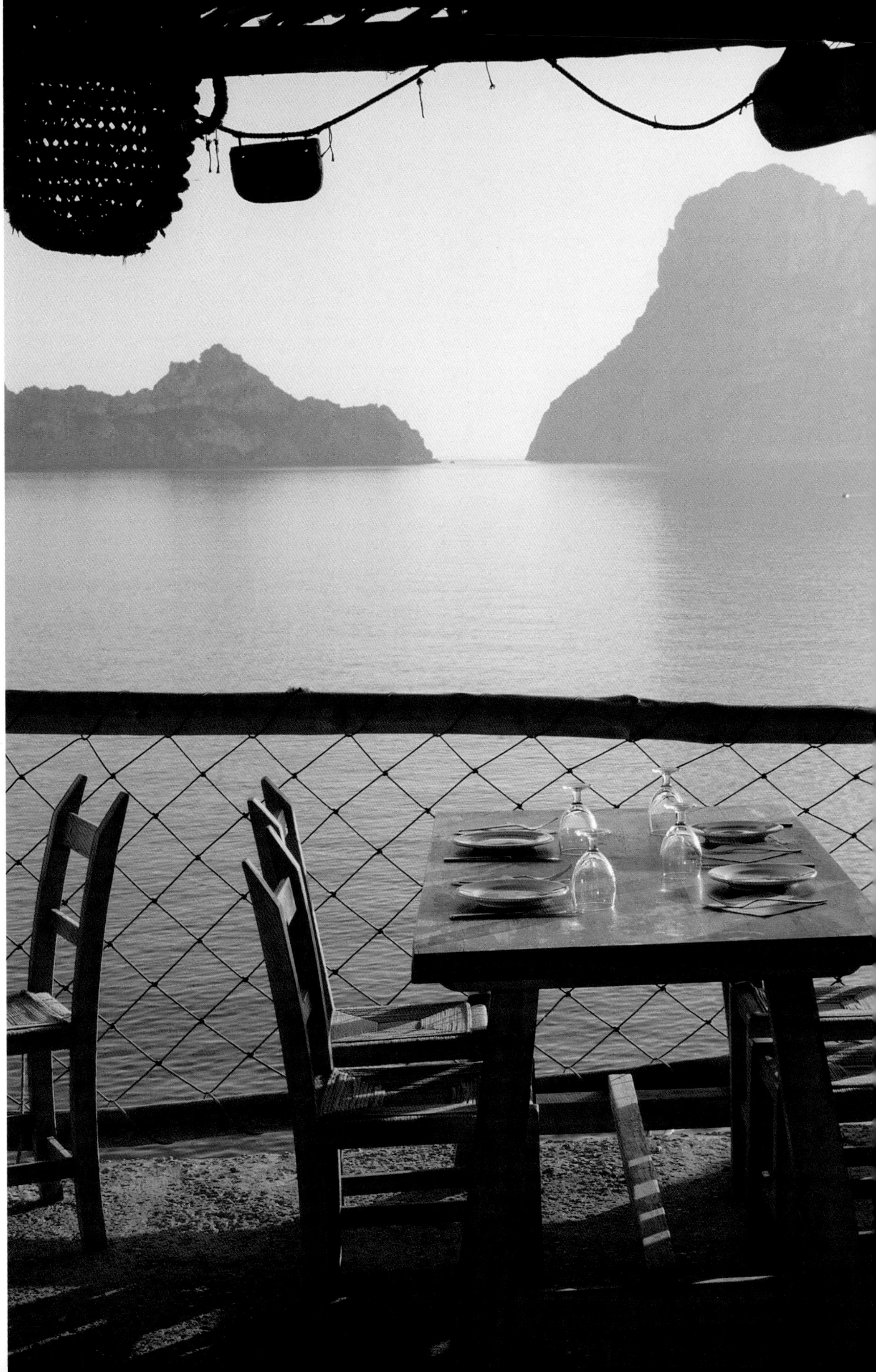

kinds of commerce and, of course, the pirates who preyed upon them. Over the centuries, a succession of invaders has passed through these islands, each one leaving its mark. One of the most substantial influences came from the four hundred years of occupation by the Moors, from 848 to 1229 A.D. They developed the first systems to exploit the islands agriculturally, building stone terraces in the mountains and complex systems for the collection of water. Eventually, as on the mainland, the Moors were expelled by the Christians: the Balearics fell to Jaime I on New Year's Eve, 1229. Finally, after periods of rule by Catalonia-Aragon, the islands became part of a new Spain in 1469.

Catalan evolved as the principal language of the islands following the reconquest in 1229. From this base, the local dialects spoken by the inhabitants have evolved: Mallorquí, Menorquí, and Eivissenc. These dialects include many words derived from Arabic and other languages, a legacy of earlier eras. Under Franco's regime, in retaliation against the resistance shown by the Catalans, it was decreed that only Castilian could be taught or spoken. As a result, most of the inhabitants of the Balearics today speak Castilian, but Catalan and its local dialects are undergoing an enthusiastic revival, and town and street names have been restored to their earlier forms. In this book, we have tried to use the Catalan names and spellings where practical. However, after thirty years of suppression, there are inevitably many inconsistencies in words, spellings, and diacritic usages.

During the early nineteenth century, the Balearics began to attract the European intelligentsia and aristocracy, but it was not until after the Spanish Civil War and World War II that tourism became a significant industry. Today, the diversity of the islands' charms and attractions is well known – but we hope that the wonderful homes in this book will give a fresh perspective on why they continue to entice visitors to their shores, some of whom never leave.

MAJORCA

ABOVE In this wild setting, a tasseled hammock slung between two native oaks promises a peaceful hour or two.

LEFT Rugged boulders jut into the waters of this half swimming pool, half rocky creek, forming the side and bottom of the pool, which was designed by the architect Antonio Obrador. The view from the paved terrace alongside is of craggy peaks bordering the valley that leads down to the sea, glimpsed in the distance two miles away.

Hidden in a fertile valley dominated by the peaks of the Puig Major lies the estate of Moncaire, enjoying a seclusion unmatched by virtually any other property on the island. A single-track road descends at tight angles through an oak forest, silent save for the flocks of sheep grazing on the dramatic outcrops of rock. Only after several bends does one catch a glimpse of the tiled roofs of a *finca*, or farmhouse, the stone belfry of its little chapel, and, under the eaves of a tower, its *mirador*, or lookout.

The house dates back to the fifteenth century and was more recently the home of the Laotian prince Champasak, but it has been completely remodeled by the present owners over the course of the past eight years. With the Majorcan architect Antonio Obrador, they have created a house that uses the traditional materials and characteristic features of Majorcan vernacular architecture to provide a comfortable family home and a place for entertaining friends. Collections of objects as diverse as Etruscan ornaments, English heirlooms, and contemporary sculptures are mixed with Spanish pictures and Majorcan furniture, giving the house a cosmopolitan, cultured atmosphere. Inside and out, the *finca* is rich in references to the island's architectural history, from the library bookcases inspired by those at Can Vivot in Palma to the magnificent *mirador* – the covered rooftop terrace with views across the valley – examples of which can be seen on houses all over the island. Honey-colored Majorcan stone and native woods have been used for doors and moldings; their distinctive graining and color give the house a sense of place. Where modern solutions have been found for remodeling this old *finca*, traditional materials set them in context.

Outside, what must have seemed an unpromising site has been turned into an opportunity, and an ambitious garden has been laid out. Part of it is on a geometric plan with rectangles of paving alternating with rectangles planted with cacti, juniper, myrtle, box, roses, and other shrubs. Beyond the garden, lush fields irrigated by the Moorish stone channels that carry water down into the valley act as a bulwark before the rocky precipices assert their dominance over the landscape. In every direction there is little sign of human habitation; apart from this remarkable house, the valley seems to belong only to the rare eagles circling high above and the somnolent lambs on the ancient terraces below them.

LEFT, ABOVE *Intriguing objects are scattered throughout the house. Here, decorating a table in the* tafona *(formerly the olive pressing room), is a fan-shaped arrangement of brass irons in place of the more usual ashtrays and dishes. The irons would once have been used for stamping patterns onto fabric.*

LEFT, BELOW *Many of the objects in the house have belonged to the family for many years. This iron circlet of rings is part of a collection of Etruscan ornaments. The dull glow reflected off its beveled surface catches the eye.*

RIGHT *The rich interior of the historic Can Vivot in Palma provided the cue for the library bookcases. Stained a deep red, they house the owners' collection of antiquarian and modern art books. The lower two shelves are in fact cabinets painted with* trompe l'œil *volumes and honeycomb mesh to resemble the shelves in Can Vivot. The library table, with its fluted pedestal, is a modern English piece, its top inlaid with exotic woods. The chairs are Italian, dating from the seventeenth century.*

LEFT *The heart of the house is a huge galleried room on the site of the* tafona, *or old olive pressing room. By raising the height of the roof, Obrador has managed to create a lofty and elegantly proportioned drawing room, well lit by a tall arched window punched in the long wall. Curtains made of woven mohair from Swaziland fall in warm folds from a massive pole, while the generously sized sofas and pictures from the owners' collection impart sophistication and grandeur to what was once a simple agricultural building.*

RIGHT *Leading up to the tower is a spiral staircase – another of Obrador's creations. Cool stone steps fan out around its central point, and whitewashed free-hand plastering provides it with a sculptural quality.*

RIGHT Following the line of the pitched roof, the windows in this bedroom climb along the eaves and give views, from a pillowed window seat, of the peak of Moncaire in one direction and the sea in the other. The bed is a modern reproduction of a traditional Majorcan design.

FAR RIGHT This bathroom has been decorated on a botanical theme by the English artist Nem Burgess, whose delicate white and green "plantings" have created a soothing atmosphere that seems worlds away from the wild surroundings of Moncaire.

Far removed from the pace of his life in New York, Hans Neuendorf's house, on the site of an old *finca* near Santanyí, exudes a serenity that is palpable. Perhaps it was a need for tranquility that prompted Neuendorf – an art dealer – to ask his friend Claudio Silvestrin, the renowned minimalist architect, to design a house for him. As Neuendorf puts it, "minimalism is soothing . . . there is no visual noise."

In a setting that at first seems quite at odds with the clean lines of his buildings, Silvestrin's large terra-cotta block lies among olive groves and a patchwork of fields at the end of a rugged track. On closer acquaintance, however, it becomes clear that this house is firmly anchored to its island landscape through its closely observed, albeit stylized, interpretation of Majorcan architecture and ideas.

In the silence of the countryside, the thirty-foot-high walls around a paved courtyard create an atmosphere that seems to recall some ancient temple. But twentieth-century outdoor living never feels far away; piercing a wall of this ascetic

ABOVE The upstairs loggia overlooking the internal courtyard has a built-in stone seat, while a small window pierces the thick exterior wall to allow a glimpse of the trees beyond.

LEFT A sharp-edged rectangle has been cut through one wall of the internal courtyard, making this dining space. Mirroring the sky, stretching for forty yards into the tops of the olive trees, the pool culminates in a cascade, spilling into another shallow pool seven yards below.

court, a clean-edged rectangle of space provides a covered dining area. The interiors, also in keeping with the minimalist aesthetic, are sparsely furnished. The massive dining table, built-in shelves, and bench seating were designed by Silvestrin and, despite the scale and monumentality of the living areas, are intended for informal, flexible use. Opening onto the patio, for example, ten-foot-high glass doors, which slide invisibly into the thickness of the door frames, instantly extend the living space outdoors.

Mallorca's strong sun plays an important role throughout the house: outside, the clean lines of the building direct it into knife-sharp patterns of sunlight on walls and floors, while inside, the small shuttered windows in a bathroom, for example, ration the sun's rays to preserve the cool air. Although Silvestrin has used Italian travertine marble extensively, he has also given the house local context by using stone from nearby Santanyí for the paving around the pool and in the garden, and by including such features as his interpretation of a Majorcan farmhouse fireplace in the dining room.

In the grounds, the dry-stone walls of the old *finca* remain, but straight stone-paved paths have been newly laid and the grass has been close-cropped under the olive trees: an inevitable collision between the order of minimalism and the unruliness of nature.

ABOVE *The kitchen area, sited at one end of the dining room, is almost entirely hidden from view by a travertine-clad island housing – and at the same time concealing – sinks, stove, refrigerator, and storage. The open layout was designed for cooking among friends and to encourage a relaxed, informal atmosphere. From the dining room, huge glass doors open onto the patio, but folding wood shutters shade the space during the hottest hours of the day.*

RIGHT *The long dining table, made from an enormous slab of travertine marble and supported by two blocks, was designed by Silvestrin. Arranged around it are oak rush-seated chairs by Hans Wegner, the same design as those in the outdoor dining area and elsewhere in the house. What seems at first to be an overhanging wall, running the room's width, turns out to be a modern interpretation of the traditional fireplace found in fincas across the island.*

ABOVE The local Santanyí stone used for this basin – a smooth hemisphere supported by a rectangular plinth – links the pure minimalist interior to its Majorcan context. The four small windows punched through the thick wall do likewise; with shutters letting in slivers of light, they echo an island type. Marble shelves divide this area from the bathtub on the other side.

ABOVE Inspired by a Japanese design, the tub, by Silvestrin, is made from broad planks of Lebanese cedar. Natural light comes from clerestory windows inserted in the far wall above

the "beams," bathing the interior in a cool light. The color and grain of the wood and the striations of the marble partition add texture to the shapes and shadows of this airy bathroom.

ABOVE The strip of clerestory windows continues from the bathroom through to the bedroom, linking the two interiors, physically and atmospherically, with their shared natural light.

The bed seems to float above an expanse of terra-cotta flooring, while on another of Silvestrin's clean-lined built-in stone benches a sculpture by Robert Graham stands in splendid isolation.

ABOVE This old door studded with iron bolts and bleached by the sun provides an unlikely hook for a little cotton shift.

LEFT An arched doorway leads from the tiny garden crowded with flowers and vines, into a shaded interior. Instead of the usual bead curtain that serves the purpose of welcoming cool breezes and discouraging flies, a delicate assembly of different lengths of strung driftwood, collected on the island's beaches, catches the sunlight.

Majorca is famous for the welcome it has always extended to the free spirits who fall under the island's spell and settle here. While many are tempted to stay on at the end of a summer vacation, it takes an adventurous spirit to turn that longing into reality. One of those who visited Majorca and never left is the Spanish artist Conchi, who lives in a simple small *finca* in the village of Calonge. In her work she responds to Majorca's essential beauty in a particularly direct way – by collecting and using driftwood, polished glass and stone from the beaches, and dried grasses and flowers from the interior. The fragments of island landscape that she turns into mobiles, sculptures, and hangings seem to document her careful and sensitive observation of Majorca's character.

The small rooms of the traditional peasant's house where she lives with her young daughter have been treated with the same delicacy and respect with which Conchi approaches her *objets trouvés*. And, besides decorating the house, her work is sometimes functional, too. In the arched doorway of her house, the beaded curtain so often seen in hot climates to keep out the bugs and let through any passing breeze is replaced by a curtain of wisps of driftwood strung together, some of which are painted the bright indigo blue found in buildings throughout the islands.

Everywhere Conchi lets the simple vernacular architecture of her *finca* speak for itself; she has not remodeled or extended it to make a more convenient home, as others might have done. Upstairs, in what was a low-beamed attic space, originally used to hang *sobrasadas* (traditional sausages) and herbs to dry, she has created a comfortable, warm living room, while throughout the house ledges and angles have been used to display her work. Parts of the rugged plaster walls and chunky staircase have been painted freehand with the same indigo blue to define the dining area or the risers on the steps. This vibrant color deftly connects Conchi's driftwood hangings to the simple interior without laboring the point and making it an obvious "scheme." The same blue has even been used outside to decorate the cans recycled as flower pots in the tiny garden, which is paved with the traditional Majorcan embedded pebbles. Here, driftwood mobiles hang from the branches, and any noise that penetrates from beyond the wall dividing this patio from the village street reinforces the fragility in Conchi's work.

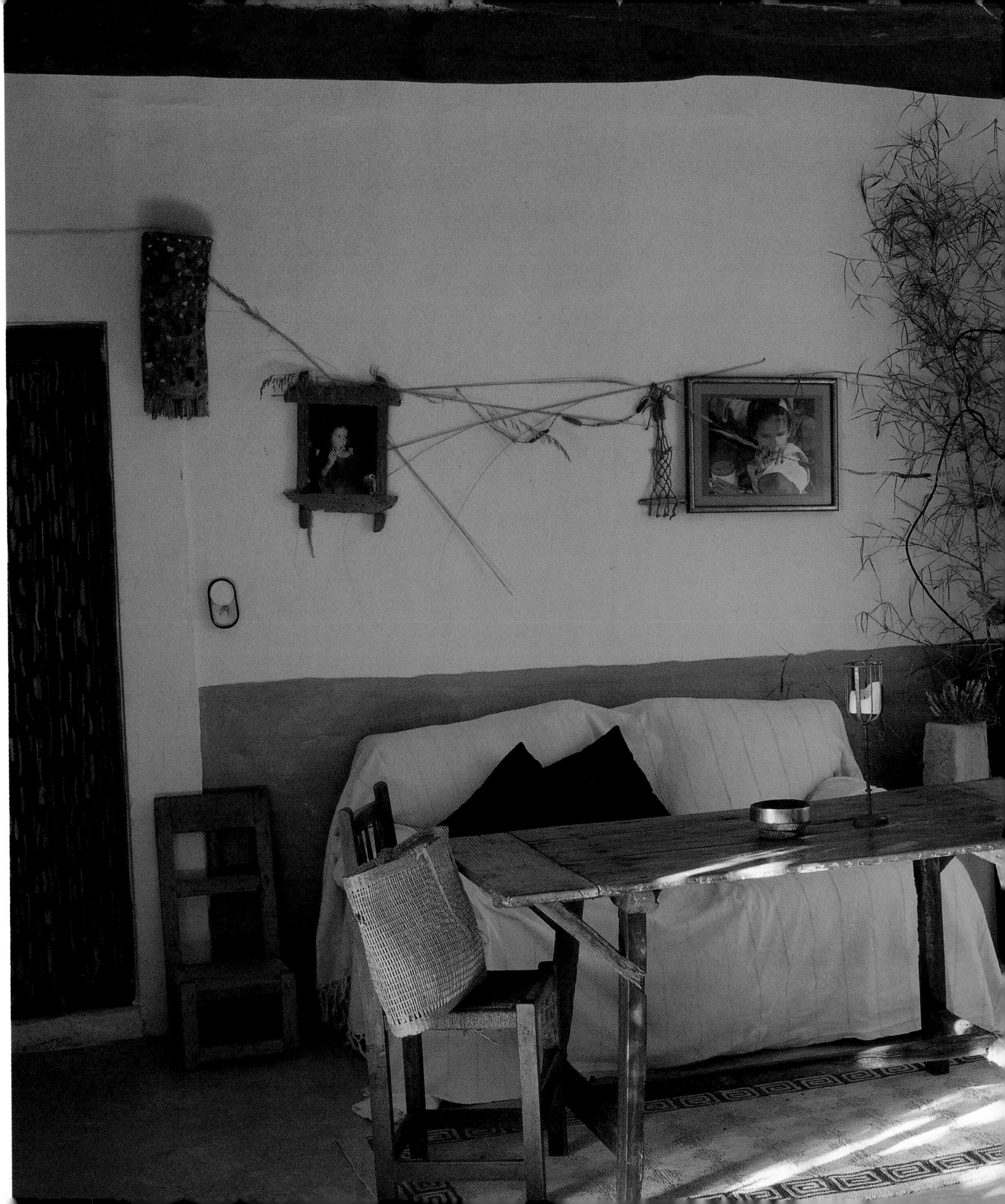

LEFT A simple interior is saved from austerity by the delicate arrangements of dried grasses and objets trouvés *and by the photographs that decorate the walls. The traditional lime-plastered walls are demarcated by an area of indigo blue that gently defines a corner of the main room. The rather battered wooden table and chairs are similar to those found in many Majorcan farmhouses, and the low chair of almost primitive construction would have been drawn close to the hearth to make the most of the fire's warmth. Another of Conchi's curtains, assembled from strands of threaded driftwood, stones, and sea-polished bits of glass which she calls* cristales del mar, *hangs in the doorway.*

RIGHT The great charm of these old farmhouses often lies in their individual eccentricities. This irregular staircase, with its risers painted blue, gives the impression that it might have been built out of children's building blocks – an association that is encouraged by the sight of a brightly painted rocking horse alongside it.

Above Hanging against an old mirror, a driftwood mobile and its reflection provide a subtle symmetrical play on Conchi's work with objets trouvés, *where no two pieces are ever quite the same. Another mobile hangs against a scarf whose tribal print makes the artist's work look like a carefully documented ethnographic display.*

LEFT *Close up, this driftwood curtain looks like a tribal necklace; the knots of string tying the feather-light twigs together also have their own strange beauty. Weathered and bleached by the sun, the door has something of the character of driftwood, too, and provides a rugged backdrop for the blue strands.*

RIGHT, ABOVE AND BELOW *Two of Conchi's delicate works of art demonstrate how she matches individual pieces of driftwood to create more formal effects in her work. Through her gift of careful observation, she seems to enjoy a close relationship with the island as she combs its beaches for fragments that are of no obvious use to anyone else.*

The purchase of Son Palou was a snap decision for its Swedish owners. They had known Majorca for many years, spending vacations on the island based in their Palma apartment. From time to time they had thought about buying a town house in the old quarter of Palma, but it was not until a friend of theirs, the Majorcan architect Antonio Obrador, introduced them to the countryside around the village of Santa Maria that they reconsidered. Then by chance Son Palou, a house that Obrador had recently completed, came up for sale and was soon theirs.

On the site of an old farmhouse in a beautiful valley setting near Santa Maria, Son Palou is that rare thing, a completely new house that nonetheless seems tied to its landscape in the most natural way. With his deep knowledge of the island's vernacular architecture, Obrador has been able to create a contemporary reworking of the traditional *finca*, laying it out for an informal, modern lifestyle. Local stone, native woods, like the stained pine used for internal joinery, and terra-cotta flooring have been used throughout, and design features, like the simple stone window surrounds that are found in many quite ordinary buildings all over Majorca, have been scaled up in size to become elegant decorative solutions in a substantial modern house.

ABOVE A bunch of fresh velvety apricots hangs from a shutter, ripening in the hot sun.

LEFT The clean lines and smooth surface of dressed stone make up the traditional door and window surrounds on the garden front of Son Palou. Plain white render borders the stone moldings; the rest of the façade is painted the terra-cotta pink of old fincas on the island. The gentle formality of the terrace paving is carried through into flowerbeds edged with clipped rosemary.

In particular, Son Palou is used for summer vacations spent with friends, so the emphasis is on outdoor living, although the line between the furnished indoors and the furnished outdoors seems to have been purposely blurred. For example, a traditional path that is inlaid with stone setts and smooth pebbles actually begins indoors as the decorative paving of the entrance hall. It then leads out across the garden lawn to an ancient stone bridge spanning a stream that is dry for much of the year. An outdoor living room loggia, open on three sides, is fully furnished in the hot summer months, as is an outdoor dining room.

With all this emphasis on outdoor living, it is not surprising to discover that the owners of Son Palou are avid gardeners and have planted the surrounding grounds with varieties chosen for their fragrance. Near the kitchen there is a vegetable and herb garden, while farther away orchards are planted with almond, carob, avocado, citrus, and other fruit trees. Elsewhere, traditional pebble-paved footpaths lead the visitor under a canopy of jasmine to a swimming pool from where there is a picturesque view of an ancient Moorish aqueduct.

LEFT, ABOVE AND BELOW A simple scheme of red and cream stripes for the curtains, pillows, and upholstery makes this living room informal yet elegant. Pillow covers of varying stripe widths are made from vintage ticking fabrics. An antique kilim rug covers terra-cotta flooring, and the doors lead onto a loggia furnished as an outdoor living room. Flowers picked in Son Palou's garden are arranged as two or three individual blooms in vases, while armfuls of foliage spill over from the pair of urns on the mantelpiece.

RIGHT Beyond a scalloped arch in the entrance hall rises the stone staircase. The freehand plastering of the Majorcan craftsmen, working on the spot without a specific "design," gives its central sinuous curves an organic quality. Wrought-iron stair rails and the old birdcage found in a Palma market add to its elegance. An eighteenth-century Majorcan chair stands on the hall's inlaid pebble-and-stone patterned floor, an example of a piece of traditional local furniture becoming a highly sophisticated focal point.

RIGHT *The fine Mediterranean weather makes this charming loggia, with its giant terra-cotta pots planted with agapanthus, the ideal outdoor living room. The lawn and a wall made of stone boulders can just be glimpsed through the haze of foliage, while in the foreground*

the orderly arrangement of chairs and tables holds promise of comfort and relaxation. An antique Majorcan sofa with elegantly curved arms has a buttoned seat cushion, rather like a mattress or yacht cushion, that was made in Palma from ticking bought in London. The lamps and wooden armchairs were found in markets on the island, while copies of the chairs were made for the terrace at the front of the house.

ABOVE A detail from the loggia showing an old Spanish tailor's worktable. Standing between two wooden armchairs with blue- and white-striped cushions, its slender proportions give it a certain elegance. Son Palou's garden is planted with flowers chosen for their fragrance; here, just a few freshly cut roses, in a frosted glass vase, perfume the air. The loggia is open on three sides so breezes keep it cool, even in the late afternoon sun.

LEFT The formal elegance of a nineteenth-century Majorcan bed with inlaid marquetry and tapered posts has been given a modern twist with a canopy of ticking fabric to match its pillows and dust ruffle. A single pink rose on the bedside table brings the scent of the garden indoors and a simple chair, of a less sophisticated design than the bed, underlines the relaxed and comfortable way in which different styles are happily combined in Son Palou.

RIGHT This small library, with scalloped alcoves flanking the fireplace, is filled with sunlight. Its wooden paneled shutters are designed in two sections, and the doors open out directly onto the garden. Above the simplest of fireplace surrounds, which forms a thin ledge mantelpiece, hangs an antique Majorcan mirror. The paintings in the room are by contemporary local artists. In this room, as throughout the rest of the house, the combination of cream curtains and upholstery, terra-cotta flooring, and the mellow colors of antique rugs creates a comfortable and tranquil atmosphere.

ABOVE *The everyday objects and toys that Miró collected are displayed all around his studio. Glimpsed from a doorway, a row of silent puppets is mounted against a deep red backdrop.*

LEFT *Miró used the bare walls of the seventeenth-century* finca *Son Boter to explore his ideas, leaving his working sketches on its walls and doorways. He originally intended to use the house as a sculpture studio, but it became a place for works-in-progress of all kinds.*

Walking into the studio where Joan Miró worked from 1957 until his death in 1983, it is as if the artist left only a moment ago. The love of shape and color that was central to the work of the Catalan surrealist painter is in evidence in every corner of the old *finca* of Son Boter and in the studio nearby, which was designed for Miró by the architect Josep Lluis Sert. Both interiors express the intensity of the creative process, not only in the collections of everyday objects that Miró used as source materials throughout his life but also in the working sketches he made on the walls of the *finca*.

Miró's ties with Majorca ran deep, although he originally lived and studied in Barcelona, then came to fame in Paris in the 1920s and 1930s, where he moved in the same circles as Picasso, Ernst, and Magritte. But Miró's mother came from the island, he had always spent vacations in Majorca, and he married a Majorcan, Pilar Juncosa. His political sympathies made life in Spain under the Franco regime uncomfortable, but, unlike Barcelona, Majorca had cooperated with Franco from the beginning of the Civil War in 1936 and was a far more stable environment. In 1955 the Mirós acquired the estate of Son Abrines outside Palma and later the neighboring *finca* Son Boter.

Miró's "dream" studio was built in the grounds of Son Abrines, just down the hill from Son Boter. His friend Josep Lluis Sert devised an enormous space filled with light from a ten-foot-high line of windows in the upper part of the north wall and from louvered top-lit panels. At one end a gallery housed Miró's lithography workshop, and at the other the wall is constructed of bare boulder stone, like a monumental dry-stone wall. A balcony opposite the windows allowed Miró to examine his larger works from a higher level while below, doors open out onto the grounds, with a distant view of the sea. Unfinished works are mounted on easels around the studio, and postcards, clippings, and sketches are pinned to its walls. Brushes and rags, color mixing plates, and pots seem abandoned on every surface among the traditional terracotta pots, baskets, chairs, and stools, poignant reminders of Miró's working methods.

After Miró's death the Fundació Pilar i Joan Miró was established, and a new exhibition building, designed by Rafael Moneo, was opened in 1986. Today this building, the *finca* of Son Boter, and Miró's studio are all open to the public.

RIGHT *Clippings, postcards, and photographs pinned to the wall of the studio designed for Miró in the 1950s by Josep Lluis Sert. This arbitrary collection of tools, objects, and visual references gives a powerful sense of the artist's creative process.*

BELOW, LEFT TO RIGHT *Paintbrushes are supported on a special frame for a work-in-progress, as though Miró might walk into the studio at any moment and pick up where he left off. The organic shapes of gourds appeared in Miró's work throughout his life, acquiring increasing symbolic importance for their associations with peasant life. The vibrant colors of his palette recall the strong, at times savage, spirit of his art.*

RIGHT *In his work, Miró drew on his Majorcan and Catalan background. In the studio he surrounded himself with the shapes, colors, and textures that inspired him, from the honey-toned Majorcan stone of its walls to the simple furniture, baskets, and hemp mats that he scattered around the huge space.*

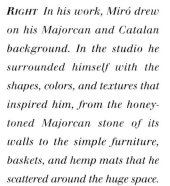

The delightful village of Deià, on Mallorca's mountainous northern coast, has been a haven and place of inspiration for artists, musicians, writers, and poets for over a century. In 1929, when Robert Graves was looking for a place where he could write, his friend Gertrude Stein suggested that he might try Deià: "It's paradise, if you can stand it." Taking her advice, Graves made his home here for many years and is buried in the tiny churchyard on the top of the steep hill in the center of the village.

Situated at the edge of Deià, where the village houses end and the ancient terraces planted with citrus and olive trees begin to climb the slopes of the mountain Teix, stands the Hotel La Residencia. Built around two old *fincas* that have been converted and extended, the property also includes a series of smaller modern buildings of traditional design which are set on the terraces behind it. The key to La Residencia's charm is the sympathetic way in which the old buildings have been converted and the new additions appear to have grown organically around them. The result is a seamless unity of style that celebrates Majorcan tradition and has a quiet, down-to-earth elegance. The hotel, which opened in the early 1980s, owes its character and style to the vision of Axel Ball, the son of a family of hoteliers who have lived in Deià for generations. It was he who masterminded the conversion of neglected buildings into this luxury hotel. Now part of the Virgin Hotel Group, La Residencia continues to build on the original ideas behind its success, earning it a reputation as one of the most picturesque and sensitively decorated hotels in the world.

In keeping with Deià's role as an artistic center, La Residencia's rooms are hung with paintings by artists such as Mati Klarwein, Yannick Vu, Miquel Oliver, and Georges Sheridan, who have all made their homes on the island. Exhibitions of work by local artists are regularly held here, as are performances of classical music in the concert salon. Throughout the hotel antique Majorcan furniture, complementing the simple airy interiors, is interspersed with traditional modern furnishings as in, for example, the recently decorated Son Fony dining room.

The natural surroundings provide drama and give the interiors their context. A terrace in front of the hotel offers seating for the spectacle provided by the setting sun, which slowly colors the jagged mountains, creating breathtaking luminous effects.

ABOVE *The familiar bright colors and fluid swirls of traditional earthenware make a decorative theme that runs throughout the Hotel La Residencia.*

LEFT *Looking out onto the lush gardens of the hotel from one of the high-ceilinged bedrooms; its uncluttered interior is furnished with old Majorcan furniture like this nineteenth-century bed. Breakfast comes on a wooden tray: a plate of fresh pastries is served with hot coffee, poured from a traditional pewter pot.*

RIGHT Set against the gray-green backdrop of olive trees below the towering peak of the Teix, the Hotel La Residencia is a mix of old and new buildings. Knitted together with the character and detailing of the original fincas *at its center, the modern additions blend well with the old. The original olive pressing room, or* tafona, *has been turned into a renowned restaurant, El Olivo, and all the swimming pools, tennis courts, bars, and cafés have been carefully landscaped so as to maintain the impression of a jumble of vernacular buildings on a number of different levels. In front of the hotel, tables and chairs are set out on the terrace so that guests can enjoy the gardens below with their palms and orange trees. From the mirador, or lookout, on the roof there are sweeping views of the azure sea far below the village.*

ABOVE Breakfast and lunch can be taken in the informal dining room known as Son Fony. Its furnishings are from Son Pax, a design company that produces traditional Majorcan furniture, fabrics, glassware, and china, but with a modern twist. Here, for example, a typical Majorcan chair design has been made in bright Mediterranean colors. Paintings by local artists are hung throughout the hotel – a reminder of the rich artistic life for which Deià is famous.

Four years ago, on an impulse, Isabel Bastidas acquired an abandoned bar dating from the 1930s. One day, driving along the main street of the picturesque town of Artà, where she had been living for some time, she spotted the "For Rent" sign; two hours later, she was negotiating with its owner. Isabel describes the subsequent renovation, decoration, and opening of her café-restaurant as a "baptism of fire." She had no formal training or experience as a decorator or restaurateur, but she did possess energy, enthusiasm, and quantities of the style and flair for which the people of her native Barcelona are famous.

In only two months she had transformed the rubble-strewn bar into a lively café-restaurant. Originally made up of a series of rather cramped, small rooms, the interior has now been opened up, but although some walls have been taken down, the original layout of rooms has been echoed in the setting out of tables and chairs in the different areas of the ground floor, which now feels comfortably spacious.

ABOVE In the garden behind the Café Parisien, the dusty ochers and pinks of peeling paint are as important to the atmosphere as the citrus trees and trailing vines under which tables are set out during the summer months.

LEFT Isabel Bastidas opened up a series of smaller rooms to create airy seating areas in her café. Each of them is furnished differently, but informality and humor run throughout. The pavimento staircase with its glass newels leads to a store guarded by a bright blue sheep.

The quirky decor reflects clearly Isabel's amused and confident eye for the unusual and intriguing. Armchairs, which she found in the garden behind the building, have been restored and positioned among a cheerful mix of old and new furniture. The focal point is the sweeping curve of the brilliant cobalt-blue bar, which is modern, as are the bar stools, designed by her brother Sergio, who also lives on the island. Above the bar hang lights with dramatic, oversized vellum shades that illuminate this striking new installation.

Instead of an overdesigned scheme, which can seem to dictate what sort of crowd the establishment expects to serve, this is decor that does not take itself too seriously. It is almost as if the interior is intended to entertain, and it certainly contributes to the informal café atmosphere of this busy and popular place, where you can come for a meal or simply to read the papers, drink coffee, and eat the fresh, fluffy Majorcan pastries called *ensaimadas*. The dining area is also an exhibition space for painting, photography, and sculpture, while a local designer recently chose to stage a fashion show here. Throughout the Café Parisien are paintings by Francesç Roca, a Catalan artist who lives in nearby Capdepera.

During warm weather diners can eat in the garden at the back, where stone walls and crumbling render make a picturesque courtyard and where the *rentador*, the old stone sink used for washing clothes, and stone *cisterna*, for storing water, remain in situ.

I sabel Bastidas, the owner of the Café Parisien in Artà, originally came to Majorca from Barcelona, where she grew up and had run a fashion store. She came to know the island through her brother, a designer, who is married to a Majorcan and lives and works here. To escape the hectic pace of city life, she and her husband moved to Majorca fourteen years ago; later they parted, and Isabel, who had fallen under the island's spell, decided to stay on and find a home for herself and her two teenage daughters.

She eventually settled on a modest house in Artà, which was in a state of total disrepair. The traces of its former use as a stable and store on the ground floor, with rooms above for the peasant family, were still visible, but it did not take long for her to transform it. With the same wit and style that are evident in her decoration of the Café Parisien, Isabel has created an original, feminine interior. Its character is in part due to the fact that she has kept structural intervention to a minimum, and the transformation has not involved a lavish remodeling or a persistently uniform approach.

ABOVE Smooth pebbles painted by Isabel's daughter – some of them made to resemble tubby toy cars – are displayed in a glass box like geological specimens.

LEFT Like the Café Parisien, the ground floor of Isabel's house has high ceilings and feels cool and spacious. Her conversion of this town house has involved minimal structural intervention; instead, she has made subtle decorative changes, like painting the glass door panels blue to create a filtered-sunlight effect.

Isabel is clearly a practical romantic; everything from the layout to the decoration has been carefully thought through. Her solution to the problem of the broken tile floors she found on her arrival was so successful that she later repeated the technique in the café. Collecting up all the intact tiles as well as the fragments, she relaid them using the unbroken ones to create and define "rooms" within an open-plan space – like the ground floor of her house. The tile fragments were then used as mosaiclike crazy-paved "carpets," and in the spaces that were left, she laid the traditional polished pebbles that are found all over Majorca. In the café, the pebble paths link the different room areas, while in her house the pebbles are laid like a path right through the house from the front door to the back garden, dividing the dining room area on the one side from the living room area on the other, both "rooms" paved with tiles.

Chance and hard work seem to have played as much a part as anything else, with furniture rescued from among other people's discards then cleaned, restored, buffed up, and given a new home. She has successfully mixed these finds with a few antique pieces, like the side chairs from Menorca, and modern pieces, like a large white sofa from the local Coconut Company, which imports furniture from Africa and the Far East. In other, less restrained, hands the effect might have been a cheerful jumble, but here the result is a seamless blend.

FAR LEFT *Running through the ground floor of the house from the front door to the tiny garden, one of Isabel's inventive polished stone "paths" divides the dining room area from the living room area. The small circular window beside the staircase is a new touch added to the old room.*

LEFT *Isabel's bedroom takes up most of the top floor, which would originally have been used for hanging herbs and sausages. The exposed stone wall gives the room a more rugged look than the rest of the house, but by painting the beams white and putting down coir matting she has made a restful bedroom. As elsewhere, Isabel has taken quite modest pieces of furniture, like the dark-framed mirror rescued from the garbage dump, and combined them to create an essentially feminine look.*

RIGHT *A smooth heavy marble holy-water basin, from a church that was being torn down, has been adapted for use as a little sink in the corner of the dining room area. Sculptural as well as useful, the terra-cotta pots it holds each contain a candle.*

ABOVE *Against the backdrop of an ancient wall dating back to Moorish times, simple garden chairs made of metal and a high-backed wooden bench furnish a cool corner of the interior garden, which lies behind the main courtyard.*

LEFT *A lofty twin-arched loggia overlooking the courtyard leads into the principal rooms of the first floor. The stonework has been stripped of its render to reveal the markings left by the original stonemason.*

J ust behind the great curving waterfront of Palma's harbor lies the historic center of this great trading city, its merchants' houses lining the winding streets around the cathedral. Twenty years ago, when all eyes were on the expansion of Palma's suburbs, it took a special sensitivity to see the appeal of the city's old center, which had become underappreciated.

Two Swedish brothers, Bosse and Leif Ljungstrom, who had, with their parents, always spent vacations in Majorca, took their father's advice and bought an old merchant's house here. Its foundations go back to Moorish times, but in its present form it dates from the eighteenth century. Like other such houses, this one has depositories around a courtyard on the ground floor and an external staircase leading to the offices and family apartments above. Architecturally the building is not elaborate, but its proportions, including the twenty-foot-high ceilings and the huge doors and windows of its upstairs rooms, give it a grandeur that the Ljungstrom brothers have respected in their treatment of its interiors.

Beyond and behind these vast rooms, stairs lead down to a series of ground-floor rooms of less intimidating proportions, with doors out onto a garden terrace. Despite the different sequences of rooms there is a unity of approach to the interiors, which combines an enjoyment of antique furniture, whether local or from farther afield, with a relish for modern design. A certain nonchalance marks the strange arrangements of pictures, furniture, and objects that have been gathered together from travels, from Sweden, and from the local Ikea store.

The brothers' keen interest in design is further evident in the scattering of furniture made by a new company set up by Leif in partnership with Agneta Cederlund; her house is also featured in this book. Called Son Pax, its aim is to harness Majorcan craftsmanship and materials, making traditional furnishings with a contemporary edge. Its furniture is made of native woods finished in bright Mediterranean colors, while fabrics in modern patterns and colorways are woven by the old family studio of Guillem Bujosa in Santa Maria. Tiles, terra-cotta, glassware, and lamps are all produced by Son Pax – and the new dining room at the Hotel La Residencia showcases its work. In an appropriate return to their commercial origins, the huge merchant's offices of the Ljungstrom house are sometimes used as a halfway station for samples and pieces from Son Pax on their way to and from trading partners.

LEFT, ABOVE AND BELOW These cream paper fans arranged like flowers in a vase might also be useful in the heat of summer. The silver boxes, cups, and bell were given to the brothers by their father, who was a jeweler.

ABOVE In the sitting room on the ground floor, at the back of the house, a twelve-foot-long sofa was specially made to fit the length of the room. Its cushion has been made like a mattress and covered in gray-blue ticking, reversed to give a softer look. One of three small folding tables that punctuate the sofa, the brilliant blue version was made by Son Pax, Leif Ljungstrom and Agneta Cederlund's design company.

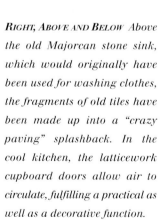

RIGHT, ABOVE AND BELOW Above the old Majorcan stone sink, which would originally have been used for washing clothes, the fragments of old tiles have been made up into a "crazy paving" splashback. In the cool kitchen, the latticework cupboard doors allow air to circulate, fulfilling a practical as well as a decorative function.

FAR LEFT *On a Majorcan marble-topped cabinet, what seems to be an almost casual assembly of pictures and objects has been put together with startling effect. A picture in the style of the cubist painter Fernand Léger is propped against the wall; viewed up close, its bold, precise composition makes it an uncanny presence behind a framed carving, a set of teeth, and some Chinese pots.*

LEFT, ABOVE *A pair of modern Ikea lights flank a Majorcan Second Empire–style bed in a room that opens off the interior garden.*

LEFT, BELOW *The two cherubs acquired by Leif during the time he lived in Sicily are mounted on a formal plinth. The basin, set into a simple sturdy shelf, is surrounded by a more eccentric collection of ornaments, which includes an exotic stuffed bird on an elaborate stand.*

RIGHT One of the vast first-floor rooms is left almost bare so that the visitor can experience the full impact of its great proportions: a large expanse of terra-cotta flooring, the imposing twenty-foot-high ceiling, and the huge door and windows. This would have been a receiving room or office when the house belonged to a merchant. The height of the windows called for the paneled shutters to be made in three sections; otherwise, their weight could not have been supported on the hinges. The blue picture by Bosse on the far wall is also made in three linked sections.

ABOVE The quirky mix of styles running through the Ljungstrom house is illustrated in the huge library, with the striking juxtaposition of a painting in the style of Fernand Léger above a more delicate arrangement of furniture of eighteenth-century flavor. Lampshades on Ikea stands pick up the brick red of the table in the painting.

RIGHT The Swedish element is never very far away, and here Leif has taken a traditional Swedish horse ornament and had it reproduced as a metal doorstop. A feather sticking out of the top of a pile of birdcages adds an ironic note to this unusual still life beneath a table of traditional eighteenth-century Swedish design.

J ørn Utzon, the celebrated Danish architect of the Sydney Opera House, has for many years had a deep attachment to the island of Majorca. In 1972 he decided to build a house for himself and his family on the spectacularly rugged southern coastline near the village of Porto Petro. Can Lis is set among myrtle and pine trees on the very edge of the cliffs, and its design and orientation are in perfect harmony with its dramatic position and panoramic views.

The house is at once strikingly modern in concept – in its position, layout, and combination of building materials – and at the same time entirely in keeping with Majorcan vernacular tradition. For example, although the roofs are flat, they are edged with the curved tiles typical of houses on the island, while the chimney caps are adapted from the pyramidal form often seen in the south of the island. Can Lis is arranged as a series of five separate buildings linked by walls and paved paths, set at slightly different angles from each other so that they open out onto different sea views.

ABOVE Four lithographs from the Matisse series "Jazz" line the wall above a drawing table.

LEFT The walls of the house are built of massive stone blocks, which are left bare in this high-ceilinged living room, like an ancient temple. The crescent-shaped sofa made of polished stone is positioned opposite three angled window openings that appear to have no frames or glass. In reality, however, the glass is tilted inward at the top, making it almost invisible.

The house is built out of large blocks of the local hard sandstone known as *piedra mares*, which is quarried and sawn nearby. Its color varies from golden to rose, or even red, depending on the light and the dampness of the weather. Used for both exterior and interior walls, the massive rectangular stones give the house – which is not large – a strange, atmospheric monumentality. Both inside and outside the walls are left bare of decoration – nothing detracts from the color, texture, and pattern of the stone and, equally, everything is directed toward the contemplation of the rock, sea, and sky that are framed as different vistas by angled openings in the thick walls. At the same time, the house seems to offer a tranquil, cavelike refuge from the elements, a place in which to reflect upon the world outside.

A great open courtyard, linked to the indoor dining area and kitchen by loggias, is used during the long, warm Mediterranean summers for eating under the stars. Its stone paving has become scarred and worn in the years since the house was built so that it seems now, more than ever, to have become a part of its landscape.

Responding to changes in the light and climate, Can Lis enjoys a close relationship with its clifftop setting and seems to have been built as a tribute to the might of its natural surroundings. There is a poetry in the rough but precisely sawn stone blocks of which it is constructed.

ABOVE *A loggia adjoining the open dining courtyard offers shade from the strong bright sun. The house is conceived as a sequence of rooms in separate buildings, which are loosely connected to each other by covered stone-paved walkways. Traditional tiles known as* tejas *have been used on the parapets, while the pyramidal chimney caps are Utzon's own adaptation of a building feature commonly found in Majorca.*

LEFT *Dramatically sited on the very edge of the cliffs on the southeastern coast of Majorca, set in scrubby vegetation, Can Lis is designed as a refuge from the elements and a lookout from which to enjoy the beauty and power of the sea. The use of local sandstone, which changes color according to the light, strongly anchors the house to a Majorcan building tradition, but its positioning, layout, and design are all modern in concept.*

Worlds away from the beaches and hotels of seaside Majorca and the rugged landscape of the island's interior is the historic city palace of Can Vivot – home of one of the oldest noble families in Palma, that of the Marquès de Vivot. It takes up almost an entire block in the oldest quarter of the city, bounded by the characteristic narrow streets that give few clues to the high-ceilinged state rooms and ornate interiors within. Can Vivot is a reminder of another age, giving a glimpse of the way of life, tastes, and culture of the island's aristocracy. The building, which dates back to the fifteenth century, was remodeled in the seventeenth century, and its interiors were decorated still further in the eighteenth century.

The grand entrance on the street leads to a peaceful courtyard paved with stone and small pebbles laid in an intricate baroque design. From here a grand staircase leads up to the second-floor rooms, which have remained virtually unchanged over three centuries. Decorated with Flemish tapestries and Italian paintings, these rooms have ceilings painted with elaborate mythical themes by Italian artists such as Antonio Soldati and Giuseppe Dardanone. In the state bedroom a magnificent canopied bed is hung with fabric said to have been taken from the field tent of Felipe V, the first Bourbon King of Spain, a gift to the first Marquès de Vivot.

The furniture with worn velvet upholstery in rich dark colors, the proportions of the rooms, and details such as the intricate door hardware all evoke the layers of history left by each generation of the family, and are evidence of different interests and patronage, achievements, and fashions. In the library, a rising tide of books threatens to obscure the painted ceiling as the *trompe l'œil* molding disappears behind the bindings. The family's nonchalance about possessions suggested by this almost cavalier approach to the decorative contribution of their antecedents brings a lightness of atmosphere to the interiors, and gives the house its charm.

Perico de Montaner, the son of Pedro de Montaner Sureda, the sixteenth Count of Zavellà, is the Director of the Archives of the city of Palma and lives in an apartment in the palace, "modernized," as he puts it, in the latter part of the nineteenth century. The author of many books about Majorca, he uses the library in Can Vivot for some of his research, carrying on his family's contribution to the cultural and intellectual life of the island.

ABOVE Seen from the grand main entrance of Can Vivot, the arms borne by Don Joan Sureda i de Villalonga, the first Marquès de Vivot, appear in polychromed marble above the grand staircase.

LEFT The imperfections of old glass in a glazed screen make the great room beyond appear mysterious and distant. Above the molding, putti play among great stucco curlicues, holding up framed portraits for the benefit of those below.

RIGHT The library ceiling at Can Vivot was painted with allegorical scenes by Giuseppe Dardanone, who also painted a retable for the altar of the Cathedral of Palma. Perico de Montaner describes this as a "family library," reflecting the interests of ten generations of his family. As the years have passed, the increasing number of books has clearly overwhelmed the dark red bookcases, and new shelving has had to be added by successive generations, with simpler stepped accommodation for the books reaching right up to the ceiling coving and even obscuring part of the trompe l'œil *architectural frieze. The crowded shelves with their long runs of mellow colored spines promise many happy hours of browsing and the possibility of uncovering long-forgotten secrets. In front of the window on top of an eighteenth-century Majorcan buffet table stand three globes, probably dating from the seventeenth century, a polychrome wood statue of Saint Michael, and a Roman head – indications, perhaps, of the range of subjects covered by the books around them.*

ABOVE *A keyhole ornament based on the cross of an ancient order of knighthood gives a hint of the richness of historical detail found at Can Vivot.*

RIGHT *Proportion rather than ornament is the key to the simple design of the library bookcases. Decoration is provided by the stamped and gilded book spines and by the rich colors of leather and vellum bindings, which are complemented by the tawny red of the bookshelves. Most of the books are on the history of the seventeenth and eighteenth centuries, collected by a family that helped to make some of that history. An antique sextant hints at the family's long association with the sea.*

ABOVE The fresh oranges stored in this wire basket provide a splash of color on a kitchen countertop above traditional lattice-front cupboards with modern brushed-steel handles.

LEFT The attention to detail in Agneta Cederlund's new house is evident in the woodwork for the doors, windows, and internal shutters. Building from scratch has enabled her to create a carefully orchestrated simplicity using white walls, wood, terra-cotta, and metal.

Agneta Cederlund's newly built house is a compelling mixture of precise design and romantic ideals. On the mountainside just above the picturesque village of Fornalutx, this small house has a wide curving terrace like the deck of a ship, which makes it appear to sail above the olive and almond trees that surround it. The view from it is of the chimneys and tile roofs of Fornalutx stretching away down a valley toward Biniaraix and Sóller. Above is the dramatic peak of Puig Major, the highest mountain on the island.

A dentist originally from Stockholm, Agneta moved to Majorca with her family in an attempt to find a simpler lifestyle. To this end, the house she has built is not large, covering under a thousand square feet, but it has been planned with meticulous attention to detail, whether in the provision of storage space, the design of door hardware, or the sensitive construction of its exterior walls; these follow the local custom of being made from found stone and assembled without mortar, like a dry-stone wall.

From the outside the house is perfectly in tune with its setting and with the old village houses of Fornalutx, but on the inside its layout is entirely modern. Traditional features, like the white plastered walls and lattice-front cupboards, are used where they work in a modern context. Agneta's feel for the colors and textures of Majorca has led her to reuse some traditional things in a new context, like the terra-cotta roof tiles converted into uplights. In contrast she has chosen stainless-steel fixtures in the kitchen; brushed-steel handles have been applied to cupboards rather than those of a more traditional style. Much of the furniture, beds, shelving, and cupboards have been built in to maximize storage space, and the bedrooms open onto the large curving terrace to extend the living space outward. There is also an outdoor kitchen and dining area, allowing the house to turn almost inside out during mild weather. Below the terrace, rainwater is collected and conserved in a huge cistern.

It is no surprise to discover that Agneta's gift for design is not confined to planning her own house. With Leif Ljungstrom, whose house in Palma is also featured in this book, she has set up the design company Son Pax, producing modern interpretations of traditional Majorcan furnishings. Throughout her house she has used fabrics and fixtures made by Son Pax that fit in happily with the antique Swedish furniture she brought with her to the island.

LEFT In the kitchen area, as elsewhere in the house, Agneta Cederlund has taken Majorcan ideas, like the softly contoured open shelving and the simple window jambs, and used them consistently throughout to give the interior a uniform modernity and a clean-lined Swedish edge. A painting by the British artist David Templeton, who lives in nearby Sóller, hangs above the plain white sofa that marks the living room area of this open-plan space.

LEFT AND ABOVE In these Son Pax ceramics a smooth cream color has replaced the patterns of banding, zigzags, and swirls found on traditional bowls and plates so that the colors and textures of fresh almonds or homemade biscuits can be appreciated all the more.

LEFT *A deep overhanging roof on the terrace provides shade for the outdoor dining area, which is used much of the year. Like everything in the house, the roof beams have been finished with simple but precise detail. The modern folding chairs that surround the rugged seventeenth-century table, as well as many other articles, Agneta brought from Stockholm. The wrought-iron chandelier above the table was made by a blacksmith in Sóller to Agneta's design.*

LEFT AND FAR LEFT A gentle discipline maintains the look of uncluttered simplicity in the bedrooms, as in the rest of the house, while a consistency of approach provides them with a decorative unity. In the main bedroom tasseled pillows, a wood-and-metal folding chair, and a modern light by Son Pax are identical to those used in other rooms. All the beds are built in, with spacious storage drawers for linen underneath, and huge Majorcan baskets are used for storage both in the bedrooms and in the space above the bathroom ceiling. The same beautifully finished olive wood window frames and paneled internal shutters are mounted in the same simple splayed jambs, and the stone sills have rounded moldings. However, the obvious care and craftsmanship with which these features have been made, with their elegant brass locks and catches, prevents them from appearing in any way mass-produced. Each bedroom of this small house opens onto the spacious terrace, instantly extending it outdoors as well as relieving any impression of the house being at all cramped.

ABOVE Spain and North Africa meet in the Winter Garden: a Persian elephant sculpture and Ben Jakober's candlesticks stand against a backdrop of Berber textiles and old Spanish tiles.

LEFT The intricate geometric carving of a traditional Islamic window screen filters the bright sunlight entering this alcove. The screens, or mashrabiyya, were made by an Egyptian craftsman for the house and can be raised or lowered to catch cool breezes or shade the room.

S et among pines on a headland that commands a view of the Bay of Alcúdia, Sa Bassa Blanca celebrates Majorca's Spanish and Moorish legacy. For artists Yannick Vu and Ben Jakober, who with the generous support of friends and patrons of the arts have turned it into the Fundación Yannick y Ben Jakober, a private foundation for the promotion of culture, the building of Sa Bassa Blanca is the realization of a long-held dream.

The sharp profile of the white crenellated walls against the deep blue sky, the gentle sound of water in the fountains, and the promise of a cool interior glimpsed through a traditional Islamic window screen make it a bewitching, intriguing place.

Based on a North African *ribat*, a type of medieval fortified dwelling, Sa Bassa Blanca was designed between 1978 and 1980 by Hassan Fathy, the Egyptian architect whose work in the vernacular architecture of North Africa is well known. Aided by two Spanish architects and craftsmen from North Africa and Egypt, Fathy was able, through the vision of the Jakobers, to revisit the distinctive architectural and decorative tradition of Moorish Spain. Together they created a dramatic and precise evocation in Sa Bassa Blanca, which is built around a traditional courtyard patio, with rooftop walkways, arched windows, and cool arcades. The decorative use of brick and the clever handling of different levels further contribute to its Hispano-Moorish atmosphere. As accomplished collectors, the Jakobers have been able to bring together inside the house not only antique textiles and furnishings from Turkey, North Africa, and Spain, but also architectural features like the Moroccan arch framing a seating alcove and the antique Spanish tiles used throughout.

The key to Sa Bassa Blanca's success is the conviction with which a traditional idiom has been used without straying into pastiche. So confident is the handling of atmosphere that while the rich textures and colors of antique furnishings shore up the sense of place in a house built only twenty years ago, the modern sculpture and paintings play a dynamic role in the scheme. A table constructed using steel reinforcing rods looks as convincing in the Winter Garden as its traditional Islamic counterpart does in a seating alcove.

The foundation's collections are displayed throughout the house and in the new exhibition building in the grounds. The serenity of Sa Bassa Blanca's lofty interiors and exterior spaces provides a setting ideally suited to their contemplation.

LEFT, ABOVE *In the gardens, as in the house, all the different cultural influences take turns to predominate. Here, English roses and clipped hedges stretch away into the distance.*

LEFT, BELOW *Against a honey-colored dry-stone wall, this battered bicycle with sculpted stone saddle is Ben Jakober's "Homage à Picasso."*

RIGHT *Sa Bassa Blanca is thought to have been the only project by Hassan Fathy, the Egyptian architect, in western Europe. Here, his distinctive reworking of the vernacular architecture of North Africa is evocative of Majorca's Moorish past. The enclosed patio garden with its marble fountains, the decorative use of wood and brickwork, the deep-set windows with their promise of cool interiors, and the terraces on different levels are all features of his style. The sharp profile of the North African–style crenellations along the exterior walls of the house seem to interlock with the blue sky; this is traditionally taken to symbolize the meeting of heaven and earth.*

LEFT The shaded alcove at one end of the patio is known as the Theatre, and has a terra-cotta-paved "stage." An Islamic diwan arch frames a ceramic tile picture by Ben Jakober from a series called "Cruxigrams." Fifteenth-century Spanish mosaic tiles, painstakingly reassembled by craftsmen, decorate the walls and front of the stage. Their dominant blue, white, and black is echoed in Jakober's art and in the cushioned bench.

RIGHT The angles and changes in level along the cool, high-ceiling passages provide many opportunities for the display of Ben Jakober's sculpture. Here a piece in oxidized bronze entitled "Greves" is mounted on a table of the artist's own design with a marble top and legs made from reinforcing rods.

LEFT The many references in the Jakobers' work hint at the range of cultural influences they work with and clearly fire the foundation they set up at Sa Bassa Blanca. A steel-mesh sculpture depicting a horse's head is from the series "Cavallo di Leonardo," inspired by the drawings of Leonardo da Vinci; another version forty-five feet high was exhibited at the Venice Biennale of 1996. The patinated bronze "Black Goddess" that stands in the entrance hall is from a series of Ben Jakober's and Yannick Vu's works entitled "Chtonian-Apollonian."

The dado decoration above it was assembled by Majorcan craftsmen using antique tiles from southern Spain; below, the walls were finished by Yannick Vu, using a powder pigment mixed with plaster which is hand rubbed with a tinted wax to produce a soft eggshell finish. This process, used elsewhere in the Mediterranean, too, gives a mottled sponged effect with a warm surface glow. On the far wall of the alcove, emphatically twentieth-century in its medium, Ben Jakober's "Fulguration III" is assembled from IBM computer circuit boards. Their repeating pattern seems to echo the geometry of Islamic decoration.

ABOVE What looks like a heroic desert portrait in the Moroccan Room has a darker message in its title, which is "Mondo Cane; Civilization in the Course of Extinction," by Gerhard Merz.

RIGHT The unique blend of East and West, ancient and modern is apparent in the smallest display of a Turkish brass lamp, a nineteenth-century European photograph of an oriental scene, and a Jakober/Vu sculpture.

FAR RIGHT The wood ceiling in the alcove of the Moroccan Room is a very fine example of fifteenth-century Andalusian craftsmanship; the archway was acquired in Casablanca and has been reassembled from an intricate series of polychrome wood pieces called maqurnas, rather like wooden stalactites. The divan seating, with its leather-covered cushions and bolsters, was also built from pieces brought from Morocco.

RIGHT Whitewashed walls and brickwork pointed arches give the Winter Garden its indoor-outdoor atmosphere. Against this roughly finished backdrop, the beauty of the intricate tile border around an internal window stands out. Assembled from small mosaiclike pieces, the seventeenth- and eighteenth-century tilework sets the color tones for the room. Below, on the divan, European floral tapestry cushions rest upon woven textile coverings from the High Atlas Mountains that were used originally as tent linings by the nomadic Berbers of Morocco. The painting by Yannick Vu portrays San Giuseppe di Copertino, the levitating monk of Italian folk legend, whose presence adds an energy to this otherwise peaceful interior. The marble-topped table designed by Ben Jakober supports candlesticks made of steel rods, and a soft light is reflected off the dull metal and gentle contours of a Persian elephant sculpture.

LEFT A corner of the Winter Garden showing the Islamic pointed arches, with their distinctive lattice fenestration. Ferns and other plants surround a Victorian deck chair, and Ben Jakober's coiled lead sculpture "Soft Touch," looking like a pottery vase, stands on a slender bronze table, while mounted on the pedestal is a bust of the artist by Giuseppe Ducrot.

RIGHT A collection of sixteenth-century Spanish pottery stands out against the sturdy shelves in the kitchen. Freehand plastering gives the built-in cupboard, shelves, and window jambs the soft, irregular contours of a traditional farmhouse kitchen. Tiles from Talavera, on the mainland, an antique refectory table from northern Spain, and a Majorcan brass oil lamp complete this airy interior.

FAR RIGHT, ABOVE AND BELOW A massive stone sink, which was once used for decanting olive oil, fills this alcove. The traditional green and white tiles and bowls are from Valencia. Elsewhere in the kitchen, ceramics and copper pans make a striking display.

Hidden in the landscape, Jean Louis Mitjans's summer home in Majorca is the perfect private retreat. For three or four months each summer, Mitchi (as he is known) takes time out from his punishing work schedule as an international film producer and director based in Barcelona, escaping to the mountain hideaway he has created above the village of Biniaraix. Built into the steep side of a ravine through which courses the stream Torrente es Barranc, the house has spectacular views down a valley to Biniaraix and to Sóller beyond. On either side of the ravine the ancient olive trees and native oaks grow on terraces built from boulders by the Moors a thousand years ago, painstakingly assembled into walls that stretch along the mountainside.

Originally drawn to Ibiza, Mitchi was so taken with Majorca on his first visit that he "changed islands." He settled on Biniaraix as a place relatively unknown to tourists, reached by a winding road leading from the narrow back streets of Sóller. The house, a ten-minute walk from Biniaraix, is inaccessible by road – like all proper hideaways – and was built stone by stone by Mitchi himself. At first he transported sand, cement, and stone by donkey, but later gained permission to use a small tractor after convincing officials that it would not damage the stone path built by the Moors up the mountain. The house consists of one rectangular room with a platform bed, like two single beds across its end, with room to sleep two people, and a living room area with platform divan seating. There is no internal plumbing or heating but, in a grotto cave on a terrace below the house, Mitchi has installed a proper bathroom with hot running water. For most of the summer, while he is here, life is conducted in the outdoor living areas where he has built a kitchen and a shaded living and sleeping area, again with built-in platforms for beds and seating covered with long mattresses. On two or three patches of terrace below the house, Mitchi has cleared the ground and sets out deck chairs under the trees at different vantage points so they look like sentries on the ramparts of some ancient encampment.

High above the valley of Sóller, Mitchi lives a simple life in the open air, leaving his lair only to buy food from the local markets and fish straight off the boats in nearby Porto Sóller, which he then cooks over an open fire for friends and family. In this idyllic setting the absence of modern conveniences is a precious restorative luxury.

ABOVE Deck chairs are set out in companionable pairs on terraces below the house. A backgammon board painted on the ground helps to while away the hours.

LEFT Mitchi's mountain home, like a primitive encampment, is camouflaged by the native oaks and olive trees found on the ancient terraces above Biniaraix. By building up the dry-stone walls constructed by the Moors in the eleventh and twelfth centuries, Mitchi has created a retreat in the wilderness.

ABOVE AND RIGHT The outdoor living and sleeping area is built into the hillside, enclosed by the dry-stone walls of the terraces. Here Mitchi has built simple platforms for use as beds and seating, and a table with inset tile fragments. Around the sides of what is little more than a primitive shelter with a bamboo roof, cane blinds are fixed to the wooden beams and can be raised or lowered according to the strength of the sun.

ABOVE On the terrace just below the house Mitchi has quite literally cut into a huge rock to create a cave bathroom with running hot water as well as a toilet. He declares, however, that he is much more likely to wash in the icy water of the Torrente es Barranc for the "charge of brutal energy" it gives him. Rushing seventy feet below the house, it provides constant comforting background noise in the otherwise silent ravine.

LEFT, ABOVE, AND RIGHT Inside the house, under the sloping beamed roof, a twelve-foot-long platform bed across one end of the rectangular open-plan space allows two people to sleep head to head, with a screen dividing this area from the rest of the 950-square-foot room. Cushions and curtains are made of the typical woven Majorcan fabric called llengua. *Mitchi's response to his surroundings has been to keep everything as simple as possible; there is electricity, but no indoor plumbing or heating. A collection of pictures of the Virgin Mary picked up from markets in Barcelona and Majorca seems to make a spontaneous assembly on the wall rather than a studied display, and candlesticks of different shapes and sizes are all for use rather than decoration.*

ABOVE The bushy head of an ornamental Chinese orange tree in the courtyard garden gives vivid color among a variety of different foliage shapes.

LEFT Seen from across a lily pond, the huge pavilion, which Antonio Obrador has added onto the house, looks like a floating raft. Furnished with antique Majorcan lemon-wood sofas, its dark green metal frame and delicate scalloped decoration seem almost invisible against the backdrop of trees.

S on Berenguer has been in the family of architect Antonio Obrador for generations, but the old *finca*, in a valley near the village of Santa Maria, had in recent times become run down. Obrador decided to remodel it to provide a comfortable family home for himself and his wife Clara, who is a painter.

Obrador is well known for his skill in transforming dilapidated old *fincas*; two other houses remodeled by him – Moncaire and Son Palou – are also featured in this book. He brings to each project a deep knowledge of the island's architecture and historic interiors, and a love of local building materials. Often drawing on humble sources, like the window moldings of ordinary vernacular buildings, for example, he reuses them on a grander scale to create houses that are substantial, but informal and elegant at the same time.

In his own house he has created rooms whose proportions and architecture are convincing and discreet. The dining room with its vaulted ceiling may be grand, and the symmetry of doors flanking the fireplace may seem formal, but the lack of ornament in door frames or plasterwork respects the character of the old *finca*. In the grounds Obrador has restored the old sheds; one is now used as an unusual open summer dining room, while the *tafona*, or olive press room, is left as it was, its press still in working order, but set with rustic furniture as an outdoor sitting room. The fifteenth-century chapel attached to the house is still in use and has undergone comprehensive conservation.

As with most houses in Majorca today, the emphasis at Son Berenguer is on outdoor living. To this end the gardens and house enjoy a close relationship, best illustrated in the new pavilion that has been built out from the Music Room between ponds bordered with billowing lavender and orange trees. Water is one of the main features of the garden and runs in stone channels that Obrador, inspired by the Moorish irrigation systems on the island, has adapted for decorative purposes. One of these lies under a bridge between the Music Room and the pavilion, making a dramatic entrance to this garden room. Like a great glass tent, rather than a conventional solarium, it has a metal frame with scalloped edges on the main verticals and along its roofline. In summer the sides can be opened to let the breezes through, but the great expanses of glass create the illusion that one is not really inside at all, and the sheep in the fields beyond the garden seem only just out of reach.

LEFT *Simple, almost austere, architecture in a new dining room makes a discreet backdrop for eighteenth-century furniture. The stone door frames and the doors themselves are a plain design, but their symmetrical arrangement gives the room a dignified formality enhanced by the traditional vaulting picked out in a mustard-gold color. The glass chandelier was made in the glassmaking atelier at La Granja, the old royal summer palace near Segovia on the mainland; the walnut dining table is Majorcan.*

RIGHT *The heavy yellow fabric used for the curtains and chairs in the warm, sunny library was woven in the nearby village of Santa Maria, in the studios of Guillem Bujosa, whose family business manufactures textiles by traditional methods. Below the French seventeenth-century mirror, a French nineteenth-century cast-iron stove keeps the room warm in winter, while in summer the doors looking onto the garden can be thrown wide open. The leather-covered chairs by the window have been in the family for generations.*

LEFT, ABOVE   *A long sunny passage on the upper floor has a simple shallow barrel-vaulted ceiling with a slim mustard-colored cornice, plain stone doorways, and doors with centered doorknobs – features used consistently throughout the house, creating an atmosphere of quiet elegance.*

LEFT, BELOW *The striped canopy curtains above this Majorcan bed have been parted to reveal the delicate eighteenth-century inlaid headboard. The built-in closet has the same glazed doors as those used by Obrador for the external glazed doors in the ground-floor rooms.*

LEFT *Beams resting on exposed stone corbels recall the ruggedness of* finca *architecture in this otherwise sophisticated interior, which features a full-length portrait of a cousin by Clara Urquijo Obrador and delicate seventeenth-century campaign desk mounted on a folding table. The curtains in the Music Room, hung from a slender wrought-iron pole by simple metal rings, are of a traditional material woven in the workshops of the Bujosa family in Santa Maria. On the walls hang a series of engravings of scenes from Italian operas. The early eighteenth-century piano has been at Son Berenguer for many years.*

The historic city of Palma is often under-appreciated by visitors to Majorca; its cosmopolitan sophistication would surprise many of those who think of Majorca as merely a vacation island of beaches and villas. Those who stay here longer come to realize that Palma, the capital city of the Balearics, is a vibrant and fashionable place to live, with a growing number of cafés, restaurants, design studios, and art galleries. Its historic center, lying in the shadows of the great gothic cathedral and the Almudaina, an official residence of King Juan Carlos, is an elegant part of the city, and it is here that Juancho and Enriqué found the perfect apartment in a turn-of-the-century house on the Plaça de Cort.

Originally occupied by a single family, the house was divided into spacious apartments about ten years ago, but Enriqué, who is from Palma, and Juancho, originally from San Sebastian, have kept many of the original features that were here, such as paneling and fireplaces, and in doing so have managed to preserve its period charm. Into this fine bourgeois interior they have introduced all the boldness and energy of modern furniture design, nothing less than you would expect of two people who until recently owned and ran an interior design shop in Palma showcasing the work of many well-known contemporary designers.

Their mix of interests is illustrated by the juxtaposition of old and new, such as an eye-catching orange sofa side by side with antique Majorcan furniture. Similarly, the walls are hung with abstract contemporary pictures by Spanish and Basque artists as well as nineteenth-century religious images. Their love and knowledge of contemporary design and of Majorca's traditions and history are keenly felt; but where most people's homes reflect some range of interest, in Enriqué and Juancho's case the contrast between the gentle old-fashioned elements and the vigorous new design is so pronounced that it gives the interior of their apartment a strange dynamic energy. Their *casita* on the mountainside above Fornalutx, in the north of the island, although a completely different world, shares this characteristic.

Now living in San Sebastian, where Enriqué has opened a new shop and where Juancho, who studied architecture, interior design, and art, has joined his family's interior decoration business, they have become, like so many of the adoptive Majorcans featured in this book, regular visitors to the island they love.

ABOVE The traditional shapes of glassware hand blown by the old family company of Vidrios de Gordiola in Algaida make a still-life composition with a dish of perfect local figs.

LEFT The balustraded terrace is paved with terra-cotta and overlooks the inside courtyard. Enriqué and Juancho have furnished it with a marble-topped bistro table found in a Palma flea market as well as two Majorcan cane armchairs painted a translucent green.

ABOVE *A collection of pieces of needlework with religious motifs for adorning church vestments, sewn in silk and gold thread, has been framed and hung on a bedroom wall. Below them the small antique chair is of a type that would have been used by women who, as Enriqué says, "sit in their doorways, talking with friends, observing the passersby" and keeping a keen eye on whatever is happening in the neighborhood.*

ABOVE *A set of old watercolors showing views of the rail station in Palma for the line to Sóller and Inca hang above this battered carpenter's worktable.*

RIGHT *The original turn-of-the-century fireplace and paneling give a flavor of old Palma to this otherwise spare interior, with its chair from The Conran Shop, minimal flower arrangement, and canvas by the Basque painter Vicente Ameztoy.*

Leaving their apartment in Palma behind, Juancho and Enriqué drive for about an hour up into the Serra de Tramuntana, the mountain range that runs along Majorca's northeastern coast, to the tiny peasant's hut above Fornalutx that they have restored and modernized. It is a world away from the busy city and offers them the chance to relax in peaceful but spectacular surroundings.

The village of Fornalutx has foundations dating back to the ninth century and the Moorish occupation of Majorca; its thirteenth-century church is built on the remains of a mosque. Famed as one of the best-preserved villages in Spain, its name derives from the lights (*lutx*) of the outdoor ovens (*forno*), which the laborers, tending the terraces above the village, could see as they returned home in the evening. It is on one of these terraces that Juancho and Enriqué have their little house; from it they overlook the mountain stream, or *torrente*, that runs through Fornalutx and, in the distance, the town of Sóller and the mountains encircling it.

ABOVE The larger of the two terraces, with its triangular cotton "sail" to provide shade, is fenced with posts, rails, and wire netting like any farm building.

LEFT Constructed from locally quarried Sóller stone, the house is set into the steep mountainside on a terrace it shares with ancient olive trees. A thousand years ago, during the Moorish occupation, these terrace walls were built using the same stone. Modern garden chairs hint at the present-day use of the casita.

Probably built by shepherds or laborers tending the olive trees and used only as a shelter, the house was a ruin when they found it two years ago, but it is now transformed into a cleverly designed *casita* with one principal room and two terraces – one at either end – shaded by triangular "sails" and used much of the year as outdoor living areas.

Many people acquiring such a hideaway would be so struck by its simplicity that they would adopt a decorative approach that reflected its rustic origins, but Juancho and Enriqué have been rather more adventurous. While respecting its landscape setting and restoring the exterior in a discreet way, they have certainly not foregone their love of contemporary design inside: the mountain hut has a fresh and zany interior, with two daybeds covered in cream crushed velvet and a quirky collection of objects scattered about.

As in their apartment in Palma, their sensitivity to traditional Majorcan things is illustrated in all sorts of ways, such as the fact that the little house is equipped for the simple life, lacking many modern conveniences and instead retaining, for example, features like the original built-in cupboard called a *fresquera* that they use for storing dishes. In Juancho and Enriqué's mountain *casita*, modern design does not stifle the impulse to get back to nature, nor does the austerity of the simple life stifle the enjoyment of contemporary design.

LEFT Between the beds is the original fresquera, *a cupboard set into the wall. Its picturesque sagging shelves are still used for storing dishes, glassware, and cooking utensils.*

BELOW *The English pine chest of drawers is in the dressing room beyond the kitchen; this piece of Ghanaian cloth would have been worn on the head to protect against the sun.*

RIGHT *The two modern daybeds in the main room are covered in crushed velvet from a Barcelona design studio. A platform loft provides extra sleeping space; the huge woven baskets are used for storage. The hardwood table under the loft can easily be moved outdoors to the terrace.*

BELOW Juancho and Enriqué are enthusiastic frequenters of flea markets all over the world. In New York's famous Sunday Market on Sixth Avenue, an old fencing mask and a baseball caught the eye; transported to this private world these curious trophies are like objets trouvés.

The *finca* of Son Rullan enjoys a dramatic position two thousand feet above the sea on the west coast of Majorca. It is a romantic, almost inaccessible place, but when the core of its buildings were constructed, in the eleventh century, the site was chosen less for its spectacular views than as a place to keep its occupants out of reach of the marauding pirates who plagued the coastal communities of Majorca.

Arrow loops still provide vivid evidence of the danger of incursions from the sea and, as a fortified *finca*, its proportions and character are somewhat different to most of its counterparts in the island's interior. For the owners, who bought Son Rullan in the early 1970s when it was little more than a ruin, this history was to become the starting point for a long restoration project. It took three years to make it habitable and an additional twenty to make it into the home it is today.

The track that climbs the mountainside to Son Rullan consists more of potholes and eroded ditches than flat surfaces, zigzagging up and around tight hairpin bends, past the gnarled trunks of olive trees ranged along the ancient terraces, until it emerges among the farm buildings and finally in front of the great weathered wooden doors of the *finca*. A stone carving of an angel's head and a cross above the doors are reminders of the monastic order that farmed the estate during the fourteenth century, but inside, the *tafona* – or olive pressing hall – has been converted into a huge dining room whose floor has been paved with the stone slabs that originally made up the sides and bottom of the enormous tanks used to store the freshly pressed olive oil. Other fragments of these stone tanks were used for the fireplace; and throughout the house, the original features of the building have either been retained in situ or reused in a practical but evocative conversion to make it work as an elegant twentieth-century home, totally at ease in its environment.

The huge proportions of its rooms give Son Rullan a rugged monumental character, and its owners have highlighted this. The ceilings of the Music Room and the dining room are more than twenty feet high, and the sloping window frames emphasize the thickness of the stone walls. The gigantic fireplace in the kitchen has benches built inside it for enjoying the warmth of a fire, laid with olive-wood logs, that is kept burning night and day throughout the winter months, when icy winds blow along the coast.

ABOVE In the tafona, *or olive pressing hall, a stone slab has been left exposed beside the door. Its crosshatched markings record the year's harvests and olive pressings; like the arrow loop above it, the stone has been retained in the careful restoration of Son Rullan.*

LEFT High in the wall of the lofty Music Room, with its huge doors and twenty-foot-high ceiling, is an eccentrically placed window with sloping frames, typical of Majorca.

ABOVE The distinctively shaped terra-cotta jars in the courtyard were used for storing wine and olive oil. Reminders of the long farming history of Son Rullan, their design predates even the Moorish occupation of Majorca.

RIGHT Like a mountain aerie, this terrace outside the dining room has panoramic views up and down the coast; from its parapet there is a vertiginous drop to the ancient olive terraces below. Where former occupants of Son Rullan kept a lookout for pirates, today it is set for dining.

RIGHT, ABOVE A traditional shallow stone sink like those seen in finca *kitchens all over Majorca was used for either decanting olive oil or washing clothes. Its rough surface is worn smooth in places, but it retains a monolithic grandeur despite its humble function. Layers of plaster and whitewash have softened the lines of the alcove above it, hinting at the gradual transformation of the building over the centuries. Stone floors, whitewashed walls, and wooden doors are the key elements in these interiors.*

RIGHT, BELOW This huge room next to the tafona *was originally used as a stable for the donkeys that drove the olive press. Converted into a lofty bedroom with a window high above ground level and wide expanses of unadorned whitewashed wall, it has retained the essential simplicity of a farm building and is elegantly but discreetly furnished. A modern open stair-case, which suggests, perhaps, the design of a ladder, leads up to a space that was once the hayloft but is now used as a bathroom and study.*

IBIZA, MENORCA, *and* FORMENTERA

ABOVE Jagged rock appears to embrace the house and terrace, whose outdoor dining area is sheltered by a simple cane canopy laid over a metal frame.

LEFT The outdoor dining area is furnished with a massive teak table supported on concrete and stone pillars, and with concrete benches around its three sides. From here there are spectacular views of the cove below the house, called Sa Foradada after the arched opening in the crumbling cliff across the water.

Boris Bruzs's memory of his first visit to Ibiza in 1957 is of a wild and romantic place, so when he returned a few years ago he set out to find somewhere that measured up to those early impressions. Near Santa Agnes, on the island's rocky western coast, he found what he was looking for: a house that had recently been started by a local Ibizan builder with whom Boris was able to collaborate to achieve the design he wanted.

Its situation is dramatic and secluded, set on a rocky outcrop overlooking a cove called Sa Foradada; the house itself appears to be enfolded by great flaps of gray rock that wrap themselves around the clean, straight, whitewashed lines of what is essentially a minimalist building. Boris was fired by the idea of integrating the house into the landscape – rather than imposing upon it – and this respect is woven into the design both on the outside and, with even more startling results, on the inside. Moving through cool uncluttered rooms with smooth white walls and white tiled floors, the rocky setting asserts itself as a series of eye-catchers. Framed by a doorway opening in the dining room, a mass of gray rock, part of the cliff into which the house is built, appears to have invaded the room as if it were a tongue of solidified lava that stopped short just in time and now forms one wall of the hallway. Its fissures and craggy surface, a reminder of the savage coastline, are thrown into sharp relief by the smoothness of the surfaces around it.

In the spirit of Frank Lloyd Wright, the orientation and layout of the house provide endless opportunities to admire the strength and beauty of the natural setting, whether it is in the configuration of the windows directing the gaze to different views of rock, sea, and sky, or in the arrangement of its terraces. Inside, where rock is incorporated into its interiors, the house invites contemplation as if it were a work of art, and in deference furniture has been kept sparse and simple, with glass and concrete used for tables and other ornament kept to a minimum. White light fixtures and switches are almost invisible, and the windows, with their distinctive black metal frames, have simple, functional blinds.

For Boris and his wife, Anne, who find this modernist simplicity "restful, cozy, and clean" and whose other homes in Eivissa, New York, and Paris are similarly minimalist in style, this house by the sea is the perfect place to unwind.

ABOVE Framed by the sea and reflecting the strong bright sun, a compressed metal sculpture by Alain LeBras stands on one of the whitewashed concrete benches that form the terrace parapet. In the bay below the house, the sea is so deep that friends visiting by boat are forced to anchor a little way off, out of sight, thus preserving the untamed isolation of the setting.

RIGHT The living room on the upper level of the house takes up the wide segmented bay window above the dining room, from which there is a sweeping view of the cliffs; the plain functional blinds are in keeping with the minimalist aesthetic. The desk is a slab of travertine marble resting on pillars of aggregate; the rest of the furniture is simple, contemporary, and unobtrusive.

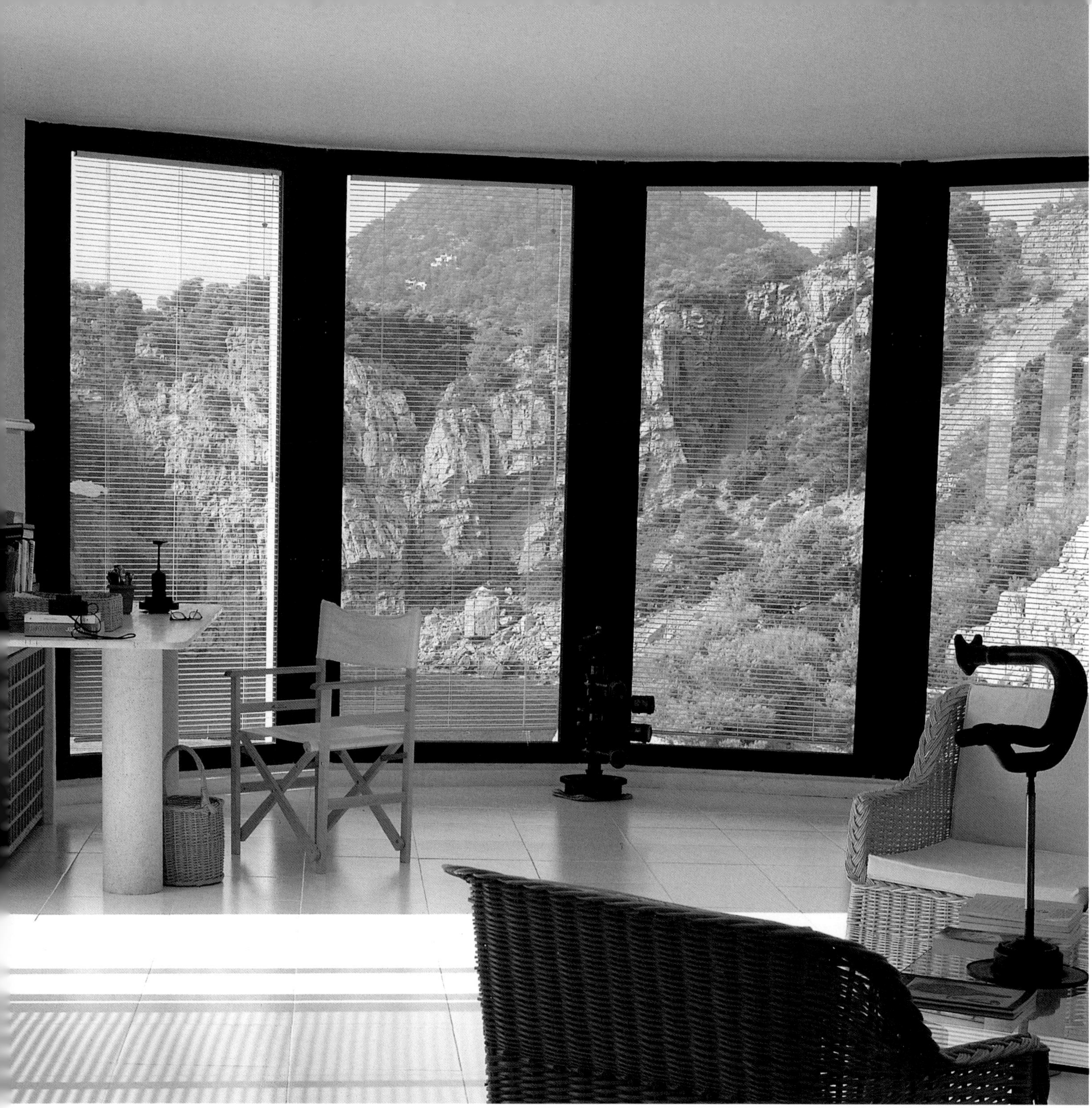

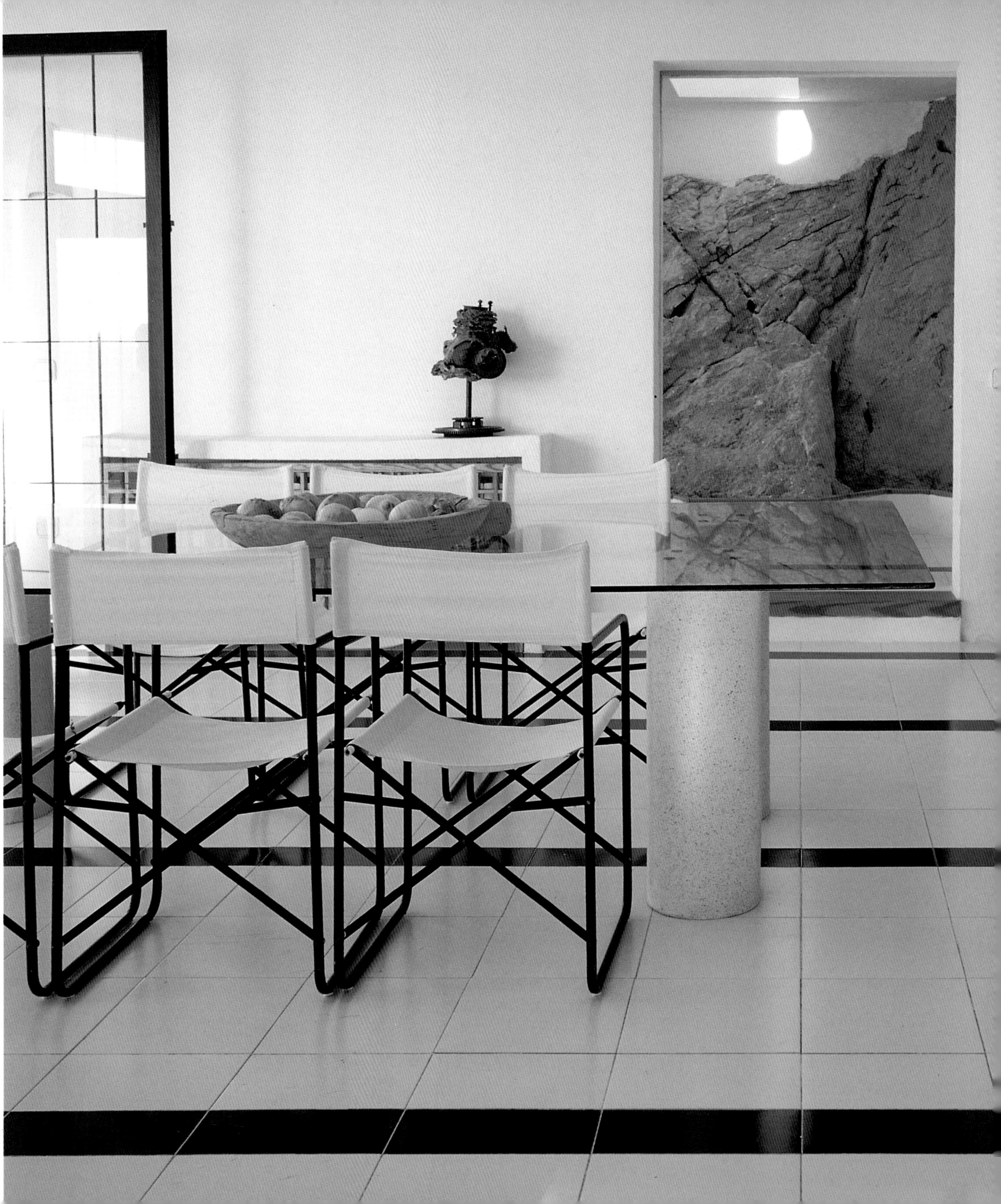

RIGHT *Filled with vegetables, this wooden tray from Kenya adds a splash of color to the barely furnished, predominantly black and white interior.*

LEFT *Beyond a simple doorway opening in the dining room, a slab of rock is an arresting sight. The building seems barely able to contain the rocky mass; its rugged beauty has replaced that of pictures and objects one would expect to see in a more conventional interior. An exception is provided by the group of handsome antique round-bellied olive jars bought by Anne from an itinerant dealer visiting the island. The rest of the room is furnished simply: modern folding chairs and a heavy glass tabletop that "floats" on pillars of concrete to a recipe concocted by Boris and his builder. The plain white decor is punctuated with strips of black floor tiles echoing the window frames and chairs.*

RIGHT, ABOVE *The rock juts into the cool horizontal lines of this guest room, where the calm and spare furnishings would otherwise give no hint of the wild coast beyond the window. Its jagged surface makes this an unconventional window seat as well as a foil to the room's understated elegance.*

RIGHT, BELOW *A bathtub, like a rock pool, has been built around another of the rocky interjections found throughout the house. Concrete grouting seals the joints and a low baseboard elsewhere protects the house from seeping water following heavy rain.*

FAR RIGHT *The use of plain white floor tiles, metal window blinds, and near-invisible downlights is continued into the bedrooms. The bed platform is clad in the same tiles as the floor and framed with the same wood used for doorsteps, ledges, and parapets throughout the house. The consistency of these elements focuses the eye instead on the natural elements, whether the dramatic coastline outside or the basket of tiny shells seen here.*

ABOVE   Found in Ibiza, the shapes of these old terra-cotta ánforas, which have long necks and two handles, and tinajas, which are squatter in form, have remained unchanged since the time of the Phoenicians.

LEFT   The familiar profile of a traditional Ibizan finca is the perfect backdrop for an exotic range of tropical plants. This part of the garden is laid out as shallow terraces, with inset rough stone "steps" leading down to the swimming pool.

From a distance, Bruno Reymond's house in the countryside near Sant Rafel looks very similar to many other traditional Ibizan *fincas.* A jumble of whitewashed cubes assembled into a house, with terraces and a flat roof, it is picturesque and simple. But Can Jordi – the old name for the place – is different. Bruno, restaurateur and owner of two furniture shops on the island, has created a house whose interior blends the simple vernacular of Ibiza with the decorative styles of North Africa, Turkey, and Indonesia to create an exotic and esoteric private world.

This eclectic mix of elements reflects Bruno's own interests: although Can Jordi is his home, he spends much of the year traveling, particularly in Southeast Asia, and his shops and home are full of objects he has brought back from faraway places. Working with such a variety of influences, it is understandable, even reassuring, to discover that Bruno has found his own personal unifying thread, which runs like a suitably solid and reliable theme through his home and the restaurant and shops that he has developed. This theme is the elephant, whose distinctive form and congenial character are celebrated in a variety of guises throughout the house, in pictures, ornaments, murals, and everyday utensils. It appears again in the names of his Bar-Restaurante L'Elephant and the two stores called La Maison de l'Elephant. Even before he moved to Ibiza five years ago, elephants held a special place in his heart and featured in the decor of the restaurant he owned in the center of Paris.

In the same way the house is filled with the sort of furniture that might be found in his shops, so his talent as a restaurateur is reflected at home, particularly in the way the house has been planned around the entertainment of friends. A series of dramatic guest bedrooms and bathrooms has been designed, each one quite different from the next in its lighting, wall treatment, and atmosphere, as well as in the different ethnic themes that have been taken as the decorative cue in each case. A gregarious man and a generous host, Bruno has designed a large living room with built-in divan seating around two walls, while outside, a huge table in the garden is set with chairs for *al fresco* eating. Stone-paved terraces surround the large pool, beside which is a Moroccan-style stone divan with a tiled canopy, the most recent building project at Can Jordi to absorb Bruno's enthusiasm and energy.

LEFT Brought back from one of his many trips to Indonesia, this hammock looks quite at home in Ibiza, slung between trees in a quiet corner of Bruno's garden.

RIGHT A massive slab of a table-top is supported by a central "crazy paving" pedestal in this outdoor dining area under the trees. Its square shape encourages communal conversation around the table. The rustic chairs, three on each side, are made of coffee wood; their joints are tightly bound with rushes instead of glue. Like the chairs, the rattan baskets, wooden bowls, and ceramic vases standing on the ground were all imported by Bruno from Indonesia. In contrast to the smooth surface of the pool edge, this corner of the garden has been paved with rough stone, giving it a rugged character complemented by the table and chairs.

LEFT A long, low platform has been installed around two sides of the living room to make divan seating. With its deep cushions, the platform provides a structure upon which the Moroccan decorative elements have been layered. Pillows covered in Moroccan textiles are strewn over the sofas; Moroccan brass lamps stand on tables and hang from the wall; and Moroccan rosewood chairs form a third side of this seating area. In the earth-colored mural by English artist Gary Cook, elephants rumble by, and a column of dromedaries stretches toward a hazy mountain backdrop in the distance .

RIGHT, ABOVE For as long as he can remember, Bruno Reymond has been fascinated by elephants and has collected elephant images of every sort. Here a silver-handled sword stick from Morocco has been given stylized elephant features.

RIGHT, BELOW This whiskey dispenser in the shape of an elephant was actually adapted for use in Bruno's restaurant in Paris, L'Elephant.

Top Glass-fronted wooden units for food storage were specially made by a local carpenter to fit the kitchen shelves.

Above Wooden spoons carved with elephants on their handles, from Indonesia, continue Bruno's theme into the kitchen.

Right The chunky proportions of the built-in kitchen, with its thick countertop and shelves, are typical of houses throughout the Balearics. Visually, they complement the architecture of the old finca, whose thick walls can be seen in the depth of the windows. An old beam running the width of the room has been painted by Gary Cook. His simple ornamental design uses a limited range of muted colors and adds a sympathetic decorative element to the plain whitewashed kitchen. Above the stove is the arched opening to the original Ibizan bread oven.

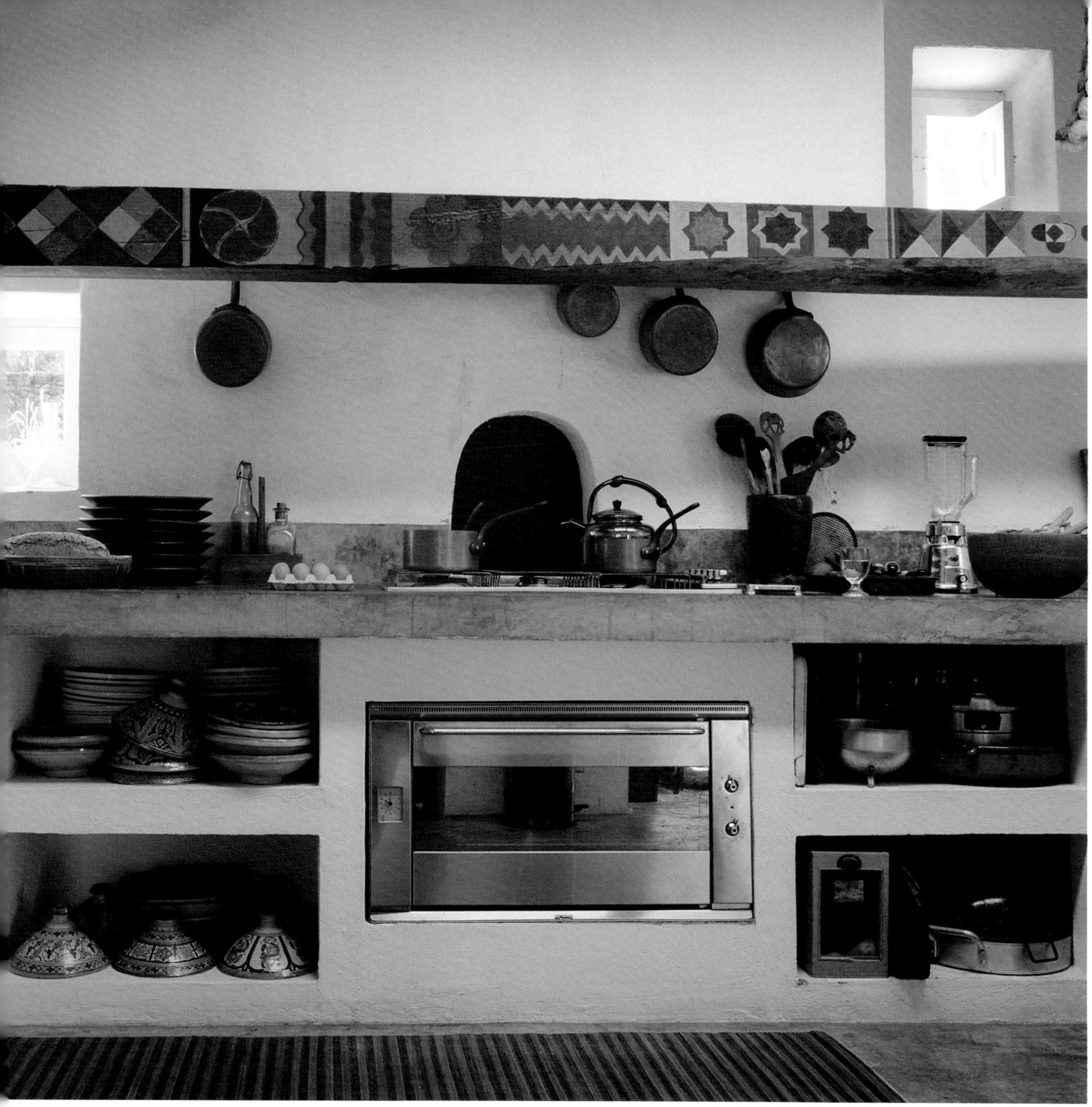

LEFT AND RIGHT The main bedroom and bathroom of the house take up the whole of the upper floor. Arranged on different levels as an open-plan space, it also has a living room area that leads onto a terrace overlooking the pool. Instead of whitewash, a sand color has been applied unevenly to rough plastered walls and the ceiling to give a textured finish and subdued light, even though the windows are larger here than in a typical finca. The cool interior is dominated by the polished cement used for the floors and built-in furniture. The scale of the sunken bath and console table with its two inset basins gives the room a monolithic solidity emphasized by the absence of applied ornament. Gary Cook's painted cupboard doors, which look like a hanging carpet and pick up all the colors in the room, are an exception to this architectural plainness. Otherwise, the decorative element is provided by the ubiquitous elephants trotting around the broad parapet of the bath or featured as a child's toy and an amusing prop in a framed bicycle advertisement.

LEFT AND BELOW This toplit bathroom is seen from the simple doorway opening connecting it to the adjoining bedroom. One of a series of themed bedrooms, this one is in a casita separate from the main house. The cast-concrete pedestal was inspired by the designs of Philippe Starck and is lined with a beaten copper basin. The walls are unevenly colored with a pale indigo wash that sets off the honey-colored stone walls and African jute hanging.

RIGHT The traditional Ibizan dry-stone wall that lines this bedroom and bathroom lends them the character of a primitive shelter, but is also a subtle color cue for the furniture and objects in the rooms and for the painted decoration that has been applied to the roof beams.

ABOVE *Outside the front door of the hotel Les Terrasses is the original* cisterna, *the main water source for the old* finca *of Can Vich, which is still very much in working order.*

LEFT *A terrace outside the kitchen is used by the family and staff for outdoor dining. The walls are washed with a pale shade of indigo, a color that Françoise has used in different contexts throughout her hotel. The original Ibizan bread oven is occasionally put to use.*

Guests asking for directions to Les Terrasses – a small private hotel in the countryside near Santa Eulalia – are told to look for the blue boulders on the roadside and turn off up an unpaved road to the old *finca* of Can Vich. This magical-sounding direction makes sense only when a huge rock painted a vibrant "Yves Klein blue" comes into view – a surreal dot on the landscape – welcoming another uninitiated visitor to the pleasures of this delightful hotel.

Françoise Pialoux, who came to Ibiza from Paris, bought the *finca* fifteen years ago, when it was little more than a roofless ruin and has personally supervised its transformation. The result is a hotel that is an informal home-away-from-home, comfortable without being ostentatiously luxurious, elegant without being stuffy, discerning without being fastidious. Françoise Pialoux's gifts as a hotelier run in her blood – her grandparents owned a hotel and restaurant outside Paris – and she says she owes much to her grandmother's teaching. Above all, it is her personal involvement in everything, from the cooking to the hotel's design and decoration, that makes Les Terrasses special. As in a private house, the hotel reflects the interests and background of its owner, being furnished with an eclectic mix of antique and contemporary furniture, and objects from the Balearics, France, and Africa, which eloquently complement the mood of the interiors. Built-in platform sofas are interspersed with comfortable chairs with slipcovers of thick fabrics in cotton or linen weave. Françoise has combined much that is Ibizan in character with elements of her own devising, such as unusual color combinations of faded blues, exposed stone window frames, and the use of bleached wood for shutters and mirror frames. However, it is not just at an aesthetic level that her design works; she has anticipated those elements that guests will particularly appreciate, like the private, individually designed patios that adjoin each of the eight guest *casitas*, built on the different levels that give Les Terrasses its name.

Outside, a swimming pool is enclosed by a dry-stone wall and surrounded by a wide stone-paved terrace where tables and chairs are set out for lunch. Evening meals are served on the terraces around the old *finca*. The cooking, like so much else at Les Terrasses, including its name, reflects the blend of French and Ibizan elements that Françoise Pialoux has so successfully combined, to create, in her words, "*Une île dans une île.*"

LEFT, ABOVE Although the old and new buildings are all based on traditional Ibizan forms and materials, Françoise has added her own design ideas such as this window frame made from exposed rough stone and the unusual straw-colored wash applied to the wall.

LEFT, BELOW Each one of the private patios belonging to the self-contained casitas has its own character. Some are shaded by creeper-clad arbors, some by cane awnings, and others by only the plant foliage.

RIGHT One of the casitas in the grounds of Les Terrasses shows a scheme of yellow walls and pale blue beams. Hand-painted flowers and foliage add a gentle femininity to the robust vernacular building, while a simple untreated board shutter at the window contrasts with the black tiles of a shower alcove behind it, imparting a strand of contemporary design into the little building. By blending these elements, Françoise has created the atmosphere of a private vacation retreat rather than that of an impersonal hotel.

ABOVE   Uneven tones in these mosaic like tiles complement the surface of a rendered wall.

RIGHT   Graduated shades of Françoise's favorite indigo are used throughout the largest of the casitas. In its living room these tones are complemented by the earth colors of the huge terra-cotta tiles and by the hessian-colored textured fabric used for pillows and curtains. Freehand plastering has brought about the characteristic arching between the roof beams.

Above *This generously sized circular basin of reconstituted stone is luxurious but understated. Likewise, the use of bleached, untreated wood for the mirror frame here and in the living room of this* casita *shows how the decoration of Les Terrasses underlines an enjoyment of simplicity. The threaded ropes of beads hung around the rooms add an ethnic element to their Ibizan character. French doors open onto a spacious terrace where guests can have their breakfast in total seclusion.*

ABOVE   Canvas curtains like sails with metal eyelets are threaded onto wire cables at top and bottom so that they can be drawn around the veranda, giving shelter from the sun. Adirondack chairs suit the New England style of the cabin.

LEFT   This simple building has been finished with great attention to detail, such as the filleted supporting posts on the upper deck. Beyond the dining table is an incomparable view of the islands off Ibiza's west coast.

H aving created a perfect "getaway" for her guests at the hotel Les Terrasses, near Santa Eulalia, it seems only natural that Françoise Pialoux should have created a hideaway for herself – a haven of peace from the everyday running of the hotel. It is perhaps a measure of her creative energy that she has not replicated Les Terrasses in miniature, which might have been the obvious thing to do, but has instead built something quite different. Finishing work at Les Terrasses, often as late as two o'clock in the morning, Françoise climbs into her car and heads west to the coast, where, after turning off the main road, she drives for twenty minutes down a very bumpy unpaved track until she arrives at what must seem like the edge of the world.

Here, clinging to the jagged cliffs and looking out toward the uninhabited islands off the coast of Ibiza, Françoise has built a cabin that is small and simple, combining the sunset views of a West Coast beach house with the restrained wooden design of a New England one. The white clapboard is in marked contrast to the traditional stone and whitewashed buildings typical of the Balearics. A deck on two levels projects from the main building and is covered by a long veranda roof, around which white canvas curtains can be drawn to give shade when the sun is at its most intense. Sliding glass doors open up the whole house for outdoor living, while inside the house is conceived as a series of open-plan spaces.

On the upper deck, contemporary deck chairs and a simple wood table are combined with old chairs, painted or covered in soft, faded blues – similar to the palette of blues that Françoise has used at Les Terrasses. Down a few steps is a smaller deck that opens off one of the bedrooms. Two red-stained Adirondack chairs are set out on the weathered boards like ringside seats for the drama of the everchanging sea and brilliant sunsets. Below the house a free-form swimming pool has been built among the rocks, overlooked by a small pool house that perches on a rocky ledge; for ocean swimming there is a steep climb down steps cut into the rock that lead to the little inlet a hundred feet below.

With only the sea and the birds for company, Françoise's cabin may be an idyllic retreat, but she is certainly no hermit when she is there: her fondness for entertaining means that friends are often gathered around the table set out on her deck above the waves.

HIGH ABOVE THE WAVES

A gigantic bougainvillea edges its way over the main façade of Can Pere Jaume, putting out its whiplike fronds toward the arches of the second-floor loggia, leaving clouds of brilliant pink flowers tumbling over the roofline and creating a natural awning over the terrace used as a dining area.

This nineteenth-century *finca* outside Santa Eulalia has been the home of the artist Grillo Demo for the past eight years. Originally from Argentina, he has lived in New York, Key West, Paris, and London, but his skills as a gardener have probably been put to best use in the grounds of his Ibizan home. When he first moved here, the gardens were a derelict wasteland – but he admits "I've always had a green thumb, even when I was a kid." The results of this natural talent are on show not only in the garden but throughout the house, which Grillo fills with vases full of bright blooms.

The yellows, pinks, and reds of the flowers find a counterpart in the interiors of the house, with the same vivid shades displayed in the furnishings and in Grillo's own painting. The line between his framed pictures and his painted wall decorations occasionally seems to become pleasingly blurred, as when a harlequin theme surfaces in a picture in the kitchen, in an abstracted diamond pattern on the wall of his studio, and yet again in a picture hanging in a bedroom. In all this, there is a sense of exuberant high spirits and *joie de vivre*, and the house appears to be filled with energy and color.

In addition to painting, Grillo has recently started to work in metal, and some of his candlesticks are displayed at Can Pere Jaume. He is also a contributor to *Interview* magazine where he presents a series on visits to contemporary artists' studios with exquisite watercolor illustrations of the studios, instead of photographs, capturing the artists at work.

Grillo's house seems to be furnished as much with the props and accessories for his painting as with conventional furniture, but despite their abundance the rooms manage to avoid visual confusion, having their own sense of order. Exotic textiles cover comfortable sofas and chairs; there are objects from India and Morocco as well as traditional Ibizan furniture and a bust of Tanit, the mythical goddess of the island. With such an idiosyncratic blend of possessions, it is intriguing to have a glimpse of the personality behind these interiors in a portrait of Grillo himself, by Julian Schnabel, executed in oils and china fragments.

ABOVE A floral theme runs through Grillo's house; here it takes the form of pattern and ornament on a Moroccan shelf.

LEFT A fine nineteenth-century carpet from Jaipur is countered by another splash of red and gold in Grillo's picture of a wheatsheaf painted on silk brocade. In the niche is a terracotta bust of Tanit, goddess of fertility and abundance, whose cult dates from the time when Ibiza was a Carthaginian colony, between 700 and 146 B.C.

LEFT Under a bougainvillea canopy, the outdoor dining area is set out around an old weathered wood matanzas table – originally used on farms as a surface on which to prepare sausages. The antique Ibizan chairs around it have pillows with Indian cotton covers; Grillo found the brass lanterns on a visit to Casablanca. The table in the foreground is made out of an old door and still has its hinges attached.

RIGHT Terra-cotta pots on the terrace spill over with color and foliage; stephanotis and jasmine climb the side of the house and drape themselves over the old wooden beams so on summer evenings the air is heavy with their scent. The great doors of the old finca are swung open, and a floral fabric valance is hung behind the opening. Above, the shady loggia Grillo calls "the VIP lounge" is set out with low sofas covered in Indian and Moroccan fabrics.

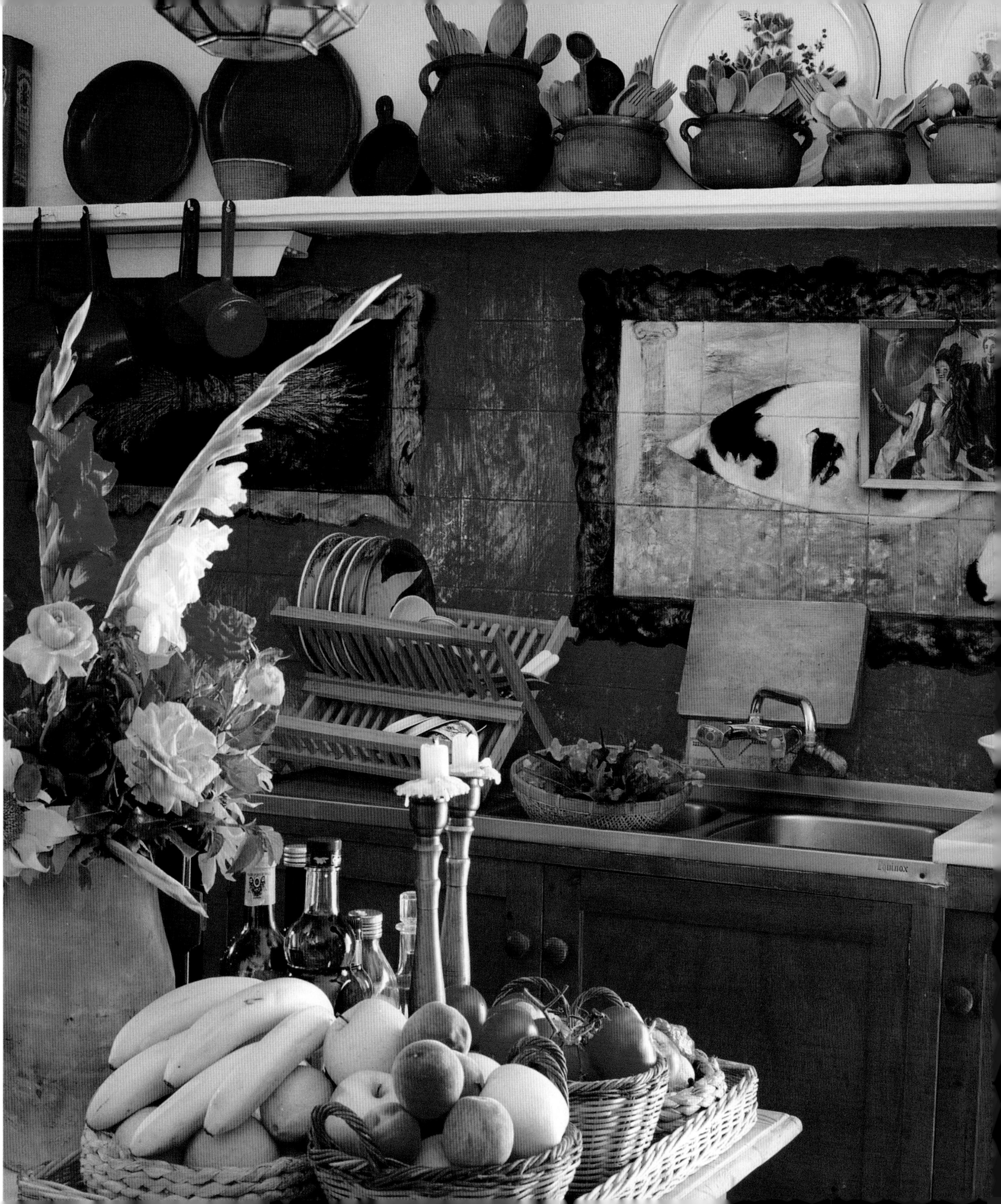

LEFT *Rather than remove the unattractive tiles he found in the kitchen, Grillo has painted onto them a gallery of* trompe l'œil *pictures against a strong red background, including another golden wheat sheaf to continue the idea of bountiful nature. This theme is also picked up in the baskets of fruit and vegetables, rose plates on the shelf, and herbs and flowers in vases. Arranged like so many more flowers in vases is a huge collection of wooden utensils in terra-cotta pots above the sink.*

RIGHT *When his "Punchinello" picture was damaged, Grillo tore off a piece of the linen, leaving a ragged edge to give the painting the wistful character of a salvaged fragment; the work now hangs in his kitchen. His spontaneity as an artist is illustrated further by the natural "frame" he has made for the picture out of bunches of dried country grasses and flowers. An old Ibizan table is home to a collection of brass Spanish church candlesticks, two of which Grillo has adorned with decorative fringes of dried red peppers like coral necklaces.*

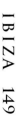

LEFT *Tracing the source of the color that is used throughout the house leads one, inevitably, to the door of Grillo's studio. Works-in-progress, sketches, and fragments give a glimpse of his methods and ideas, with flowers and butterflies the most obvious natural elements from which Grillo has taken inspiration. On the wall he has painted the diamond motif of the harlequin's costume, which appears in other contexts throughout the house.*

RIGHT *Indian and Ibizan elements are combined in this bedroom, which also includes an oil by Grillo developing his harlequin theme in a darker color range than elsewhere. The nineteenth-century Ibizan bed has an Indian woven cover, and portraits of nineteenth-century maharajahs, brought back from India, hang on the walls. In the foreground stands one of Grillo's wrought-iron candlesticks, recently exhibited in Eivissa, London, and Paris.*

ABOVE Wooden figures on an Indonesian table chart Victor's travels in Madagascar, Cuba, and Guatemala.

LEFT In the hallway dining room, Victor has arranged an apparently casual assembly of huge Spanish ánforas, furniture picked up in the South of France, animal horns, and a giant shell. These juxtaposed elements make a theatrical display, and their shared tawny coloring pulls the interior together in an unobtrusive way.

V ictor Esposito's home in the Sa Penya quarter of Eivissa, the capital of Ibiza, is a treasure trove of the exotic and the unusual, displayed with a combination of grand gesture and lightness of touch. In the tradition of the *Wunderkammer*, or cabinet of curiosities put together by gentleman collectors in the sixteenth century, Victor has filled the rooms of his house with objects he has found while trawling the flea markets of the world. The natural and the manmade, the artistic and the workaday are displayed together; the only common link between them is that at some point, whether in Guatemala or Barcelona, Tunis or the Caribbean, they caught Victor's eye and were shipped home to his apartment.

Growing up in Marseilles, Victor has very early memories of sifting through stalls in flea markets and peering into antiques shops. He developed an eye for design and decoration that led ultimately to opening his shop in Ibiza. Its quirky name – Pan con Tomate, bread with tomato – which refers to the ubiquitous food of the Balearics, hints at the highly individualistic mix of antiques, ethnic furniture, and singular objects that it sells and with which his own home is furnished. Among them he also sells work by artists living and working in Ibiza and the other islands; there are wrought-iron sculptures by Grillo Demo (whose house is also featured in this book), lampshades of natural fibers by Emiliano, and works in glass and metal by the English artist Tom Dixon.

Victor's apartment occupies two floors of one of the typical whitewashed town houses that line the narrow streets in the old fisherman's quarter of Eivissa. Though charming, these houses can feel cramped, but Victor has opened up the warren of rooms so that his is filled with light. An upstairs entrance hall doubles as a dining room, and an open staircase against one wall leads up to an airy loftlike room. This is lit on one side by a skylight and on the other by floor-to-ceiling glass doors leading out onto a sunny terrace overlooking the rooftops.

Although the layout and spaciousness give the apartment a contemporary feel, Victor has emphasized many traditional features. There are typical small windows punched through thick walls as well as larger modern openings, shallow alcoves with Moorish arches, open staircases, terra-cotta floors, and everywhere the traditional white lime plaster that gives built-in features the rounded, irregular contours characteristic of Ibizan interiors.

ABOVE Victor has a gift for bringing simple things together in an imaginative way. Here, he has reused an old stone animal water trough as a basin and made an unusual splashback by setting a few antique tiles into cement. Instead of being part of an overall design laid close together with just a thin line of grouting between them, these tiles from the Barcelona flea market can be appreciated like individual little pictures hanging on a wall.

ABOVE Old Spanish rice sacks have been used to cover pillows in a bedroom. The rough texture and natural color complement the other vegetable-dyed and woven textiles better than any modern fabric could ever do. A Moorish-style window alcove with its built-in seat is one of the few instances where an architectural feature has a part in creating an exotic interior – a role more prominently played by furnishings and trophies, such as these African spears.

RIGHT In addition to collecting objects from all corners of the globe, Victor is interested in contemporary artists. Here a wrought-iron candlestick by Grillo Demo stands beside a nineteenth-century Ibizan chest. In addition an oil painting, also by Grillo Demo, is propped up against the wall so it "belongs" more naturally to the eclectic mise en scène of elephants and other objects dotted around rather than hanging by itself in splendid isolation.

LEFT   The glass and metal sculpture on the mantelpiece is by Tom Dixon; the architectural feature above it is a chimney cap found in an old ruined finca. *Victor liked its design so much that he has had it reproduced, using it as an ornament on top of the stair balustrade seen in the picture to the right.*

RIGHT   Opening up the roof and installing skylights has created this huge loftlike space. An expanse of whitewashed wall adds to its airy feel and makes a great blank canvas against which the furniture and objets d'art *stand out sharply. Most prominent of these is the dramatic silhouette of a bull, familiar to travelers in Spain as a roadside advertisement for a popular brandy. Like many of Victor's treasures, it takes on a new life plucked from its familiar context and becomes a witty piece of "found art." Below it a collection of seats from around the world includes an Indian howdah, or elephant saddle, an African stool, and an Adirondack rocking chair that has, unusually, found its way here from Cuba.*

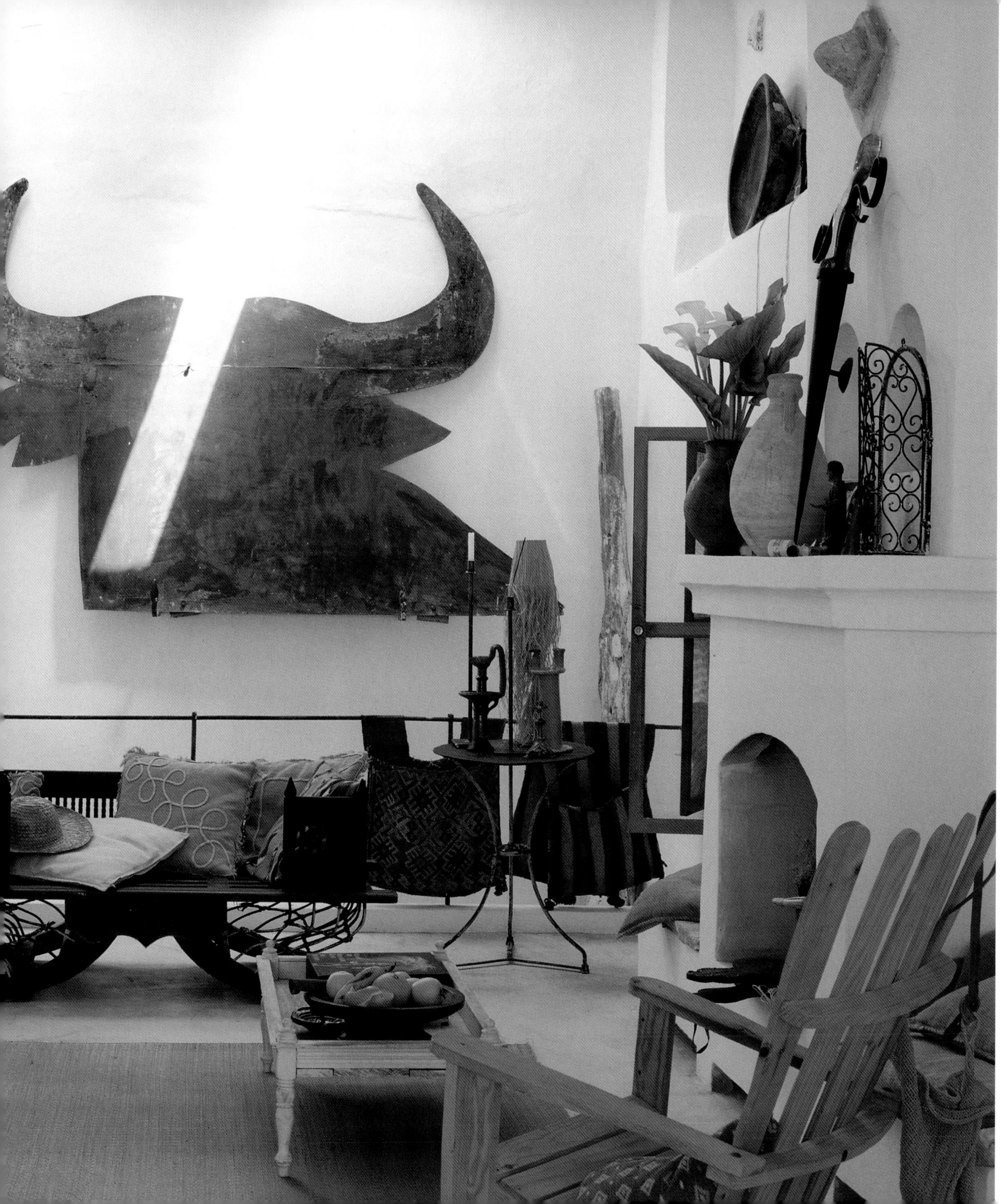

RIGHT In the living room, two weathered metal tables with delicate bases and tops, which were brought back from France, are used for displaying groups of artifacts. This arrangement includes a parchment-covered lamp by Marcelo, an artist working in Ibiza, a model of a classic Brazilian boat called a jangadeir, a glass flask, and a wooden box from Indonesia. Although the sepia photograph of American Indians by Curtis and an early view of Wall Street hanging above a group of Tunisian terra-cotta jars are worlds apart in their purpose and provenance, nothing seems out of place in this Ibizan room.

FAR RIGHT This collection of highly individualistic candlesticks seems to prompt questions about the obvious differences in their designs, much as a museum exhibit would do. The contemporary raffia lamp, by Emiliano, provides a wry note.

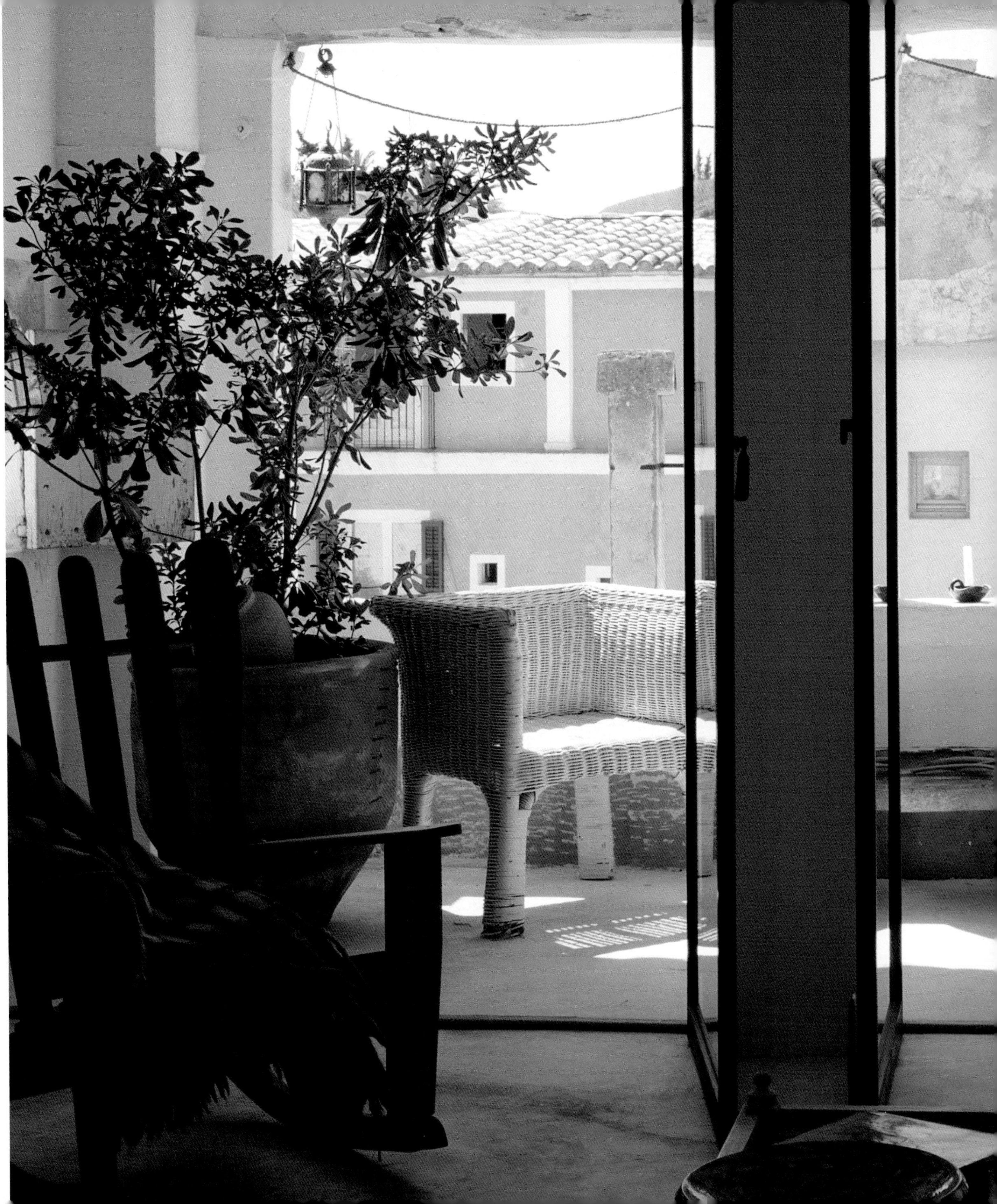

LEFT *From the top-lit living room, two pairs of glass doors lead out onto the west-facing terrace overlooking the rooftops of the old town of Eivissa. The view is framed by a white-washed parapet and a wall projecting at either side; the terrace is an intimate space furnished with painted rattan chairs and plants in terra-cotta pots. An old zinc stand-up bath hangs on the terrace wall ready for use; all that is needed is a pitcher of water for an invigorating, economical scrub.*

LEFT In the kitchen Victor installed an old brass faucet mounted on its original carved stone back, which he found in a house that was being knocked down, adapting it for use above a pair of traditional stone sinks.

RIGHT High in the wall, a pair of tiny arched windows are a wonderful example of a Balearic tradition that recalls the island's Moorish past. Like the rest of the apartment, the kitchen has almost completely unadorned whitewashed walls; Victor's collection of pots and bowls makes up the decoration. Set on the table is a tajine dish from Tunis, and Ibizan ánforas are displayed on the shelf above. Traditional lime plaster has been applied to the shelves and alcoves, giving them a sculptural quality that is missing from conventional kitchen units. Tiled countertops of a brilliant blue, terra-cotta flooring, and Ibizan peasant chairs complete the picture.

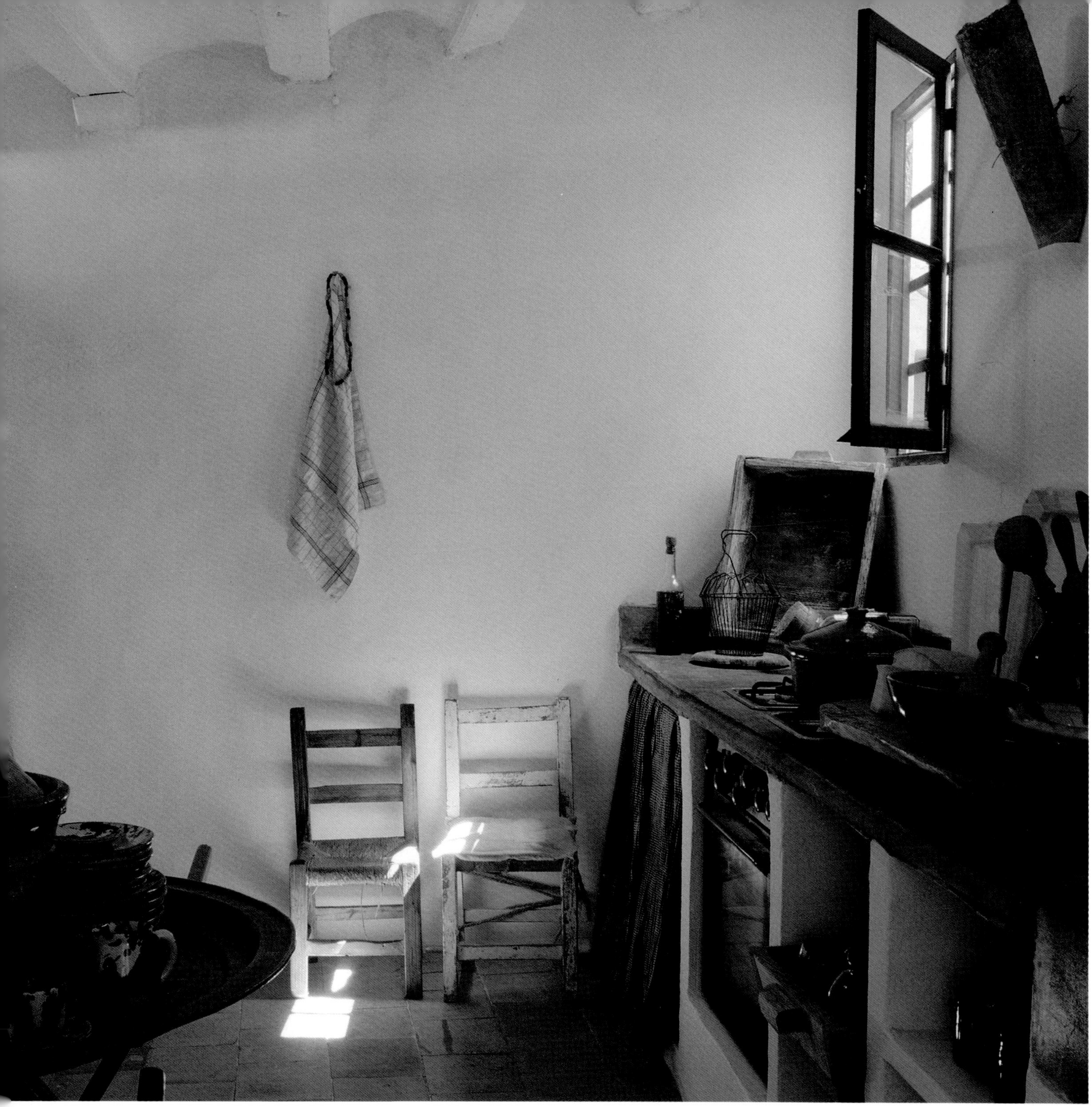

The brilliant whitewashed profile of Luis's house stands out sharply against a backdrop of billowing trees in the countryside near the village of Santa Gertrudis. A typical Ibizan *finca*, its rounded contours have been modeled by the regular application of a traditional lime plaster, which seems to give its cubic structure an almost organic form. Flat roofs and terraces with obelisk-shaped supports on their parapets carry a simple arbor of riven beams. There are low doorways and squat windows through thick walls, each opening a dark shape in the white façade, and a simple gate made of weathered stakes leads to a small patio.

Can Casa Llarga has been Luis's home for fifteen years. Originally from Barcelona, he has lived on the island for many years and has come to love rural Ibiza, in particular for the wildflowers and plants that grow here. His interest in their traditional uses and healing properties is evident from the bundles of drying herbs and flowers that hang from the old beams of the *entrada*, or entrance hall. His botanical interests are only part of a deeper appreciation of the island's natural resources, demonstrated by the way he has harnessed the sun's energy to supply electricity to his home. Huge twelve-volt batteries are installed under built-in sofas, off which all the appliances in the house are run.

In keeping with his commitment to sustainable living, Luis has done little to alter the original layout and structure of the *finca*, leaving its simple interior almost intact. Where he has put in modern plumbing and bathrooms, he has also added an unrestrainedly vibrant color scheme. His enjoyment of bright colors is evident throughout the house in the ethnic rugs and pillows he has brought home from his travels.

Rather than conforming to the straitjacket of a premeditated decorative scheme, the interiors of Can Casa Llarga are expressive of its owner's lively and continually developing interests. Tribal sculptures and works by artist friends are set out in an informal, almost haphazard way. Likewise, the furniture is a relaxed mix of modern pieces made by local craftsmen and the simplest Ibizan tables and chairs.

An idiosyncratic and uncontrived blend of ideas runs through the decoration of Can Casa Llarga, leaving the visitor with the impression that its owner is sensitive to the island on which he lives and listens reflectively to what it has to teach him.

ABOVE The cubic forms and terraces of a typical Ibizan finca *retain a strongly Moorish flavor that can be traced right back to the Arabic occupation of the island from the eighth to the thirteenth centuries.*

LEFT Here on a roof terrace that opens off a bedroom, an almost iridescent indigo called Azul de Montserrat *has been used for the parapet instead of the usual whitewash. Weathered doors and a simple chair capture Can Casa Llarga's rural charm.*

LEFT A rough plank door has been given a gray-blue wash through which the characteristic knots and graining of the wood can be seen. Beyond, in the living room, hangs an oil painting by a Japanese visitor to Ibiza in the 1930s. A desk made for Luis by an Ibizan friend stands next to a built-in sofa covered in brightly colored cushions. The antique oil lamp, found in the house, is still in use.

RIGHT Luis has retained much of the original structure and layout of the finca, *like the traditional* hogar, *or fireplace, with its great bell-like chimney, the base of which is visible here as a huge square space enclosed by beams. Practical modern additions include the smaller metal hood over the fire and the insertion of glass skylights in the flat roof that lighten what was once a dark room.*

ABOVE Exploiting the decorative appeal and charm of everyday implements, Annick has bunched together these old-fashioned wire salad baskets as if they were a string of balloons.

LEFT A small living room next to the bedrooms is furnished with a nickel-plated shaving stand, a cupboard that Jean and Annick found in the Marché aux Puces in Paris, and a Napoleon III–style daybed with pillows and mattress in mismatched stripes.

Jean and Annick first discovered Ibiza in the early 1970s, when they visited the island on their honeymoon. They were immediately hooked; from then on they returned every summer, renting houses in different parts of the island and getting to know it well. It was not long before the idea of buying a place of their own began to grow, and when they eventually came upon Sa Font Blanca, near San Jose, they knew the ramshackle, dilapidated old farmhouse could be their dream project.

Sa Font Blanca sits on the side of a hill overlooking the valley of Benimussa and its almond and olive groves. For almost four years they spent their summers restoring, decorating, and furnishing the house. Originally a *casa de labranza*, a simple farmhouse, Jean and Annick were careful to work with only traditional Ibizan building materials, such as the native hardwood called *sabina* and traditional dry-stone walls, so the house is in keeping with similar vernacular buildings. Iron bedsteads, furniture, and household articles were sought out in the Marché aux Puces in Paris and on expeditions to village markets the length and breadth of France. On each visit to the house, they loaded the car with their latest acquisitions and took the ferry across to Ibiza. What they could not find in France came from the island's antiques shops, including Pan con Tomate in Eivissa, which belongs to their friend Victor Esposito, whose house is also featured in this book.

The furnishing of Sa Font Blanca expresses the happy convergence of two approaches to collecting: that of Jean, who is a Parisian antiques dealer, and that of Annick, whose taste is for quirky everyday objects such as old-fashioned kitchen utensils. The combination has made the rooms of Sa Font Blanca both comfortable and interesting. The furniture itself is mostly of the nineteenth or early twentieth centuries, with pieces in the Arts Décoratifs style mixed with an eclectic collection of ornaments, ethnic textiles, ceramics, and baskets. Wrought-iron chairs, tables, and daybeds are used inside and out, and are fitted with cushions, bolsters, and mattresses covered in cotton fabric with stripes of different widths and colors.

Winter and early spring are Jean and Annick's favorite seasons: the Ibizan countryside is at its most beautiful, but the evenings are cool enough to enjoy a log fire. During the summer months, the house is filled with children and friends, with everyone gathering for leisurely meals around a big table set out on the terrace.

ABOVE A row of metal hooks from an old butcher's shop has been installed in the kitchen; the wire baskets hanging from it provide a practical way of making sure air can circulate around onions, the string of dried peppers, and the bulbs of garlic stored here. A wickerwork bull's head seems to preside benignly over this decorative assortment of implements and vegetables whose dark shapes are sharply outlined against the pristine whitewashed wall.

LEFT *Mixing French, Ibizan, and Moroccan elements, Annick has created an ordered but welcoming kitchen. By having drawers and cupboard doors made to fit the traditional Ibizan plastered counter, she has made a clean-lined work area that she has then filled with utensils from French country flea markets and ceramics from Morocco. French nineteenth-century wrought-iron garden furniture brings the sunny outdoors into the kitchen.*

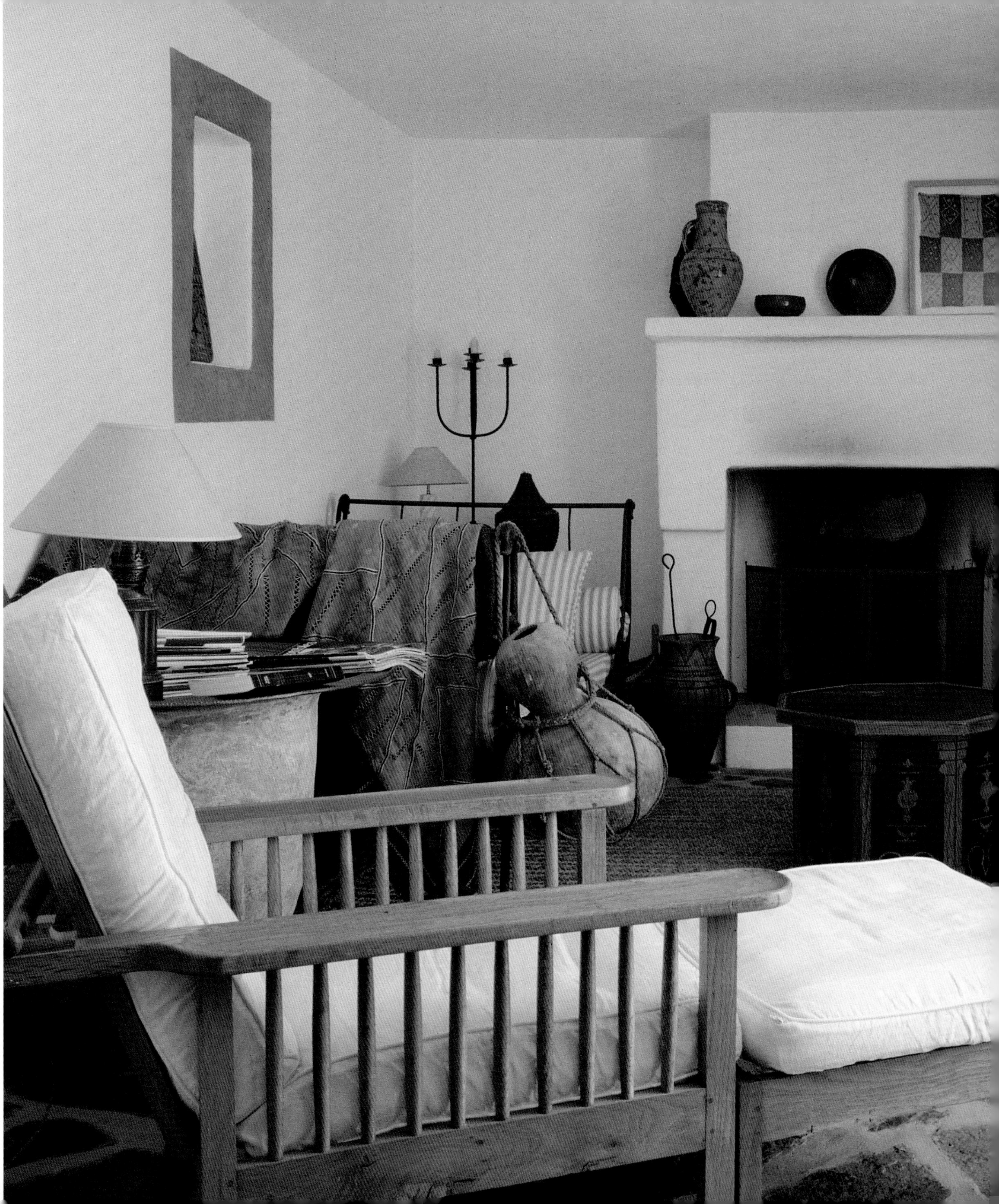

RIGHT *This nineteenth-century polychrome tablet, originally used as a demonstration sample in a Moroccan ceramics school, is displayed in its own niche with a painted ocher "frame."*

LEFT *In the winter living room, the simple, elegant design of the fireplace with its chunky proportions, blunt profile, and high mantelpiece provides a focal point around which is arranged an eclectic selection of seating. A nineteenth-century wrought-iron daybed is used as a sofa and, like others in the house, was bought in France. Opposite, Moroccan cushions are arranged on a wooden platform, and in the foreground a stripped pine English steamer chair has been fitted with white cotton-covered pillows. Braided rush matting covers the stone floor and the painted ocher frames for a niche and a window pick up the earth colors of Berber pottery.*

LEFT Against the traditional dry-stone exterior walls of Sa Font Blanca, a French wrought-iron bed has been set up with plenty of bolsters and pillows for comfortable, shady siestas.

BELOW The culinary colors of the Mediterranean: the peppers, tomatoes, and zucchini in this basket form the basis of one of Annick's ratatouilles.

RIGHT A gnarled pillar of the local hardwood called sabina – which has been used for centuries in Ibizan houses for doors and lintels – supports the roof shading the terrace outside the main bedroom. The old wicker chair and metal table, like much of the other furniture, were brought over from France by Jean and Annick.

RIGHT The satisfying shapes and muted colors of painted African baskets and boxes arranged together on a table distract from their more mundane purpose as storage for various bits and pieces. Beyond, the flamboyant Italian gilded mirror on the bathroom wall, found in a Paris market, seems to be quite at home in this purposefully plain interior. The sink itself is cast and finished to resemble marble and was made by a local craftsman in the village of Jesus. The cupboard below it has modern, but traditional, latticework doors to allow air to circulate, while the old door in the foreground has been reused in a new context. Jean and Annick have skillfully incorporated elements like this throughout the house.

LEFT A corner of the bedroom is brightened by a collection of embroidered bags from India. Decorated with buttons, mirror fragments, and tassels made from threaded shells, they hang from hooks on the wall. Below them sits a Syrian photograph frame and a basket of ethnic jewelry from Africa, the Maghreb, Turkey, India, and Pakistan. The result of Annick's passion for collecting is a house filled with objects that have become decorative by dint of being displayed together. The success of this scheme is partly due to the plainness of the white-washed interiors. These isolate and highlight the splashes of bright color or unusual shapes that her collections form on the tables, shelves, and walls throughout the house.

Brilliant colors from a constantly changing palette make Karel Fonteyne's house, near Alaior in the center of Menorca, an exotic place. La Tortuga is both his home and an informal guest house, and its layout and decoration have evolved in response to its owner's creativity.

As a photographer and magazine art editor, Karel spends his life working with images and visual effects. At La Tortuga he brings together this professional expertise and confident eye for creating striking color combinations with the impressions and possessions he has gathered on his regular and lengthy travels around the world.

The exterior of La Tortuga is painted a brilliant cerulean blue, instead of the traditional whitewash, announcing its maverick presence in the flat Menorcan landscape. This is only the first of many exhilarating surprises as the interior of the house unfolds in a sequence of luminous colors, from indigo blue, through dusty rose pink, cool pistachio, pale olive green, lemon yellow, to tangerine.

ABOVE In an interior courtyard, a cantilevered stone staircase provides shade for a Moroccan daybed laid with an antique tea set that Karel found in the bazaar in Marrakesh.

LEFT Sunlight filtered through a cane awning creates the illusion of a giant brush stroke across the bright blue wall of the terrace where guests can take breakfast. Antique lanterns and a sculpture made from recycled metal by the Menorcan artist Alfonso Murat share the space.

In recent years Karel has imaginatively converted and extended his home, creating a series of guest bedrooms and bathrooms, each with their own private entrance. In the decoration of each one Karel has explored the essence of a place he has visited through his use of color: the effect is startlingly evocative. In the African Room, for example, he has combined a hot ox-blood red with mottled olive-green walls and a yellow bedcover, which conjure up the images and colors of tribal art. African ornaments and other furnishings shore up the atmosphere like props on a stage, but the colors are the key to its success.

Throughout the living rooms and library Karel has arranged an eclectic mixture of artifacts and found objects from Africa and the Mediterranean, and the juxtaposition of ornaments and furniture is sometimes as dramatic as the unusual color combinations. Hanging on the walls and propped up on chairs and tables throughout the house are examples of his own photographs, including some taken from his book on Africa, *Black Earth*.

In the spacious yellow kitchen, which is lit by a great skylight, Karel, who is as inventive a chef as he is a decorator, prepares meals that combine the flavors he has discovered on his travels in Mexico, India, and the Far East. His guests enjoy the results of his gastronomic research at tables set out on the terrace, overlooking a garden shaded by fig trees.

LEFT In the living room the walls are colored an uneven pale violet, which seems to mimic the effect of drying plaster. Cool blue tiles are used for the floor and white paint is used for furniture and window frames, making an unusual visual link between them. As a counterpoint to the exotic color scheme, the furniture is a mix of the whimsical and the robust: a bow-fronted chest with curlicues and ornate handles is a contrast to the plain upholstery of the bench and armchairs.

RIGHT The sea is never far away in the decoration of the living room. An entire cabinet is filled with Karel's collection of shells, starfish, and sea urchins found on beaches from Mexico to the Mediterranean. On the long sideboard sit shell-encrusted boxes and picture frames, as well as a ship's lantern that belonged to his grandfather, a Belgian sea captain. The old trunk belonged to a great-aunt who was a governess on ocean liners, while an oar is casually propped against the wall and a battered piece of driftwood hung as "found art" beside it.

LEFT Odd shoes washed up on the beach are a familiar sight. Gathered by Karel like the shells he also collects, they take on a new life when arranged together, in a quite different context, above his fireplace. Karel's eye for texture, color, and drama has produced startling "compositions" such as this throughout La Tortuga. Battered, bleached, torn, and mysterious, his collection of "orphan footwear" has become an unconventional, intriguing decorative element.

RIGHT The curved and raised open hearth in the library is painted pistachio green and stands out from the indigo-blue walls. Its bell-like hood has a sharply defined molding at its base that forms a mantelpiece. The two black-and-white photographs are by Karel; the one on the left is from his book about Africa, Black Earth. *Exhibitions of photographs, paintings, sculpture, and lithographs by artists who live on Menorca are regularly held at La Tortuga. In front of the fireplace stands a classic Swedish Modern chair dating from the 1970s.*

LEFT A view from the African bedroom, with its olive-green walls, shows the adjoining bathroom, painted a warm ox-blood red. Combined with the "tribal" basin pedestal made from a hollowed tree trunk, the colors used are sharply evocative of Africa. The basin itself is made from the local piedra mares; its textured surface contrasts with the elegant chrome fixtures.

RIGHT, ABOVE The bed in the African Room is constructed out of beams recycled from the ruined finca that Karel has remodeled at La Tortuga. Its yellow cover continues the theme of hot colors used in these interiors. The local cement tiles on the floor are a shade of saffron while the wall above the bed is painted flat black. On the shelf above is a collection of animal horns found in the fields around the finca.

RIGHT, BELOW Menorcan chairs made of olive wood have seats woven from upholstery webbing, and a woven African tablecloth thrown over an old table has a handpainted tribal motif.

RIGHT In the blue bathroom of the Harlequin Suite, the shower partition stands out as a block of yellow with a diamond harlequin pattern, in the same blue as the walls, painted over it freehand so that it resembles a design painted on fabric. A bright yellow window frame and flowers in a vase add further splashes of color. The basin is made of piedra mares.

FAR RIGHT In the Harlequin Bedroom, Karel has devised a scheme of turquoise-painted furniture and yellow walls while a checkerboard pattern is taken up in the black-and-white tiled floor. An unused doorway, painted a contrasting green, has been made into a niche for an armchair. On the wall hangs a self-portrait by Helda Fonteyne, Karel's sister, and overhead a Venetian chandelier brings to mind the famous Carnival.

The design of Drew Gladstone's house, which he built himself stone by stone, was influenced, he says, by both Gaudí and the cartoon stories of Asterix the Gaul. This unlikely combination has resulted in a wonderfully idiosyncratic building that seems to grow out of the rocky terrain of Formentera, the flattest and smallest of the Balearic Islands.

Vulnerable to attack from marauding pirates, the island was sparsely populated for centuries, and even as late as the 1950s it was primarily a destination for day trips by ferry from Ibiza. When Drew Gladstone first arrived here thirty years ago, there were few houses and no roads. For his house, he chose a site on Formentera's highest point, which is only about three hundred feet above sea level, but from where he has views of Sa Mola at the other end of the island and panoramic views of the sea around the Cap.

The first part of the house to be built was a cavelike central living room with exposed stone walls and apparently randomly positioned small windows. A more diffused light also reaches the ground floor through an opening in the upper floor, which is lit with conventional windows. Fieldstone has been used everywhere – for the floor, walls, and fireplace; and the living room's main piece of furniture is a cushioned bench, a projecting lump of the rocky outcrop on which the house is built.

From the beginning of the building project Drew took care to avoid damage to the environment. He likes to say that no trees were killed to build his house; instead the beams were reclaimed from ruined buildings. Nor did he want the house to intrude on the natural landscape, which explains his choice of fieldstone for the walls. As the years have gone by, the house has evolved organically, with Drew adding rooms onto the central core, one by one, up to the current total of seven. The building is heated with two fireplaces, one in the living room and another in the kitchen area, which is the only part of the house with whitewashed walls. In the cooler months a wood stove provides additional heat while, in the spirit of sustainability, solar power is harnessed to provide electricity.

Drew's house is a poetic and practical response to the landscape of Formentera – a personal expression of sympathy for its character and integrity that he has developed slowly and reflectively over the many years he has known the island.

ABOVE The kitchen area is sited at one end of the living room; above its fireplace Drew has constructed a bread oven of a traditional Balearic type. Throughout the house he has used reclaimed sabina or juniper-wood beams.

LEFT Drew built this house with his own hands, and its curving walls, the design of its fireplace, and the organic form of the stone sofa all owe a debt to Gaudí and Drew's other muse, the cartoon character Asterix.

ABOVE Built on different levels, as tradition dictates, the cubic design of the house provides a constant drama of light and shadow as the sun moves across the sky. In the foreground, an alcove housing a shower on the sunbathing terrace is reminiscent of a North African building.

LEFT The fireplace in the high-ceilinged, spacious living room has been designed with open sides and on a bigger scale than is typical, in keeping with the proportions of the room.

or aficionados of the Balearics, the appeal of Formentera is the feeling that it is one step more removed from the bustle of modern life than neighboring Ibiza. When the owner of this house on Formentera first visited Ibiza in 1958, there were few cars and few roads, but Formentera was still more primitive. As Ibiza's popularity grew, the tiny unspoiled islet off its south coast became the obvious place of retreat for this Parisian, who aimed to spend four months of the year here in order to offset the stress of his busy city life.

Rather than adapting an old building, he decided to create a new house just ten yards from the sea. Until recently the islanders would never have lived in such an exposed position as they would have been vulnerable to pirate attacks. Started in 1970, completed in 1974, it took another ten years to bring the house to its present state. In keeping with Balearic vernacular tradition, its design is based on a series of cubes on different levels, connected by short runs of stone steps. Flat roofs and the rounded contours of corners, parapets, and moldings around doors are typical of both Formentera and Ibiza; reflecting the Arabic influence in the building, these elements are all used in a convincing modern context. Where the house departs from tradition is in the use of contrasting colors on some of the exterior walls, rather than the ubiquitous brilliant whitewash, and in the series of large picture windows that give the oceanside façade, in particular, an atypical exterior elevation. The owner says that these windows, which flood the house with light, give him "energy," and certainly the view of the sea, so close that it seems within reach, is exhilarating.

Inside, the house has a spacious, light interior open to the roof, with clean sawn beams in place of the rough-hewn timbers more commonly encountered. In the airy living room is a modern interpretation of a traditional fireplace, with its huge whitewashed hood and flue contrasting with the exposed stone of the adjoining walls. Careful attention has been given to ecologically sustainable and practical energy supply, with solar panels powering the house's electricity, and low-demand lighting and appliances installed throughout. Rainwater, always a precious commodity in the islands, is collected on the flat roof and channeled into a cistern for storage. In almost every aspect this house expresses the ideals of modern living in its layout, design, and site while respecting the style and context of the island landscape.

ABOVE In general, decorative art and ornament are kept to a minimum in a house where the sea is a constantly changing spectacle. Here, though, a piece of driftwood washed up by the waves is hung on the bedroom wall, where its fragile branches, like wire, catch the light.

RIGHT A hammock in the living room has been positioned so one can enjoy the sea views through picture windows that are an unexpected element in the otherwise traditional exterior of the house. An occasional tug on a pull-rope provides just the right amount of gentle motion to enhance hours of relaxation and reflection. When the sun is low, simple white cotton curtains can be drawn for shade, and in the winter an old cast-iron stove provides warmth.

BELOW Midnight blue was chosen for these walls since the owner believes that dark colors make a bedroom restful. Under the draping of a mosquito net, lulled by the soothing sounds of the sea just outside the window, sleep comes easily, restoring energy and calming the mind.

193

This book is not meant to be a travel guide, and the following listings certainly do not pretend to be a thorough directory of the hotels, restaurants, shops, and places of interest in the Balearic Islands. Instead, they are a collection of notes on places visited by the authors whose style and character is particularly in keeping with the houses shown in the book. Most of the hotels and restaurants listed are of modest or average prices. If they are more expensive, we think it is proper to alert you to this by using descriptions such as "luxurious" or "exclusive."

Telephone codes: the national code for Spain is 34, and the local one for the Balearic Islands is 971. All calls must include the latter code as well as the six-digit number, even if made within the islands.

MAJORCA

Hotels

Finca Can N'Ai
Cami de Son Puça 50, Sóller
tel 971 63 24 94 fax 971 63 18 99
A small hotel in an old *finca*,
with a lovely restaurant set in
the midst of orange groves.

Gran Hotel Son Net
Puigpunyent
tel 971 14 70 00 fax 971 14 70 01
An historic manor house in a
mountain village that has been
transformed into a small five-
star hotel with fifteen rooms.

Hostal Baronia
c/Baronia 16, Banyalbufar
tel/fax 971 61 81 46
A small group of houses set in
the middle of the countryside.
The restaurant on the terrace
has a wonderful view.

Hostal Borne
c/Sant Jaume 3, Palma
tel/fax 971 71 86 18
A traditional hotel, dating
from the turn of the century,
which has recently undergone
a complete restoration.

Hotel Costa d'Or
Lluc Alcari, near Deià
tel 971 63 90 25 fax 971 63 93 47
An unpretentious hotel in the
village of Lluc Alcari with a
superb location perched on
cliffs above the sea.

Hotel Es Moli
Deià
tel 971 63 90 00 fax 971 63 93 33
A large hotel built on the
terraces just outside Deià.
Great views from the pool.

Hotel d'Es Puig
Es Puig 4, Deià
tel 971 63 94 09
A small hotel built on a hill
in the heart of this village.
There are just eight rooms –
two with terraces – and
a small swimming pool.

Hotel Formentor
Bay of Pollença
tel 971 89 91 00 fax 971 86 51 55
Established in the 1930s, this
grand hotel has a glamorous
past: Monarchs and movie stars
are among its former guests.

Hotel Hermitage
Ctra. Alaró a Bunyola, Orient
tel 971 18 03 03 fax 971 18 04 11
A haven of peace nestled in an
inland valley near the lovely
village of Orient.

Hotel La Residencia
Deià
tel 971 63 90 11 fax 971 63 93 70
A luxurious hotel in a
breathtaking location within
a village renowned as a haven
for poets, artists, and writers.
The hotel has sixty-three
rooms, four pools, tennis
courts, and two restaurants.

Hotel San Lorenzo
c/San Lorenzo 14, Palma
tel 971 72 82 00 fax 971 71 19 01
A typical townhouse that
has been transformed into an
intimate yet comfortable hotel
with just six rooms.

Palacio Ca Sa Galesa
c/Miramar 8, Palma
tel 971 71 54 00 fax 971 72 15 79
A seventeenth-century *palacio*
that has become a luxurious
"bed and breakfast" with a
roof terrace and, in its vaulted
cellar, a "roman pool."

Pension Playa
Cala Santanyí
tel 971 65 41 02
A *pension* on the beach that is
set away from the crowds.

Pension Villa Verde
c/Ramón Llull 19, Deià
tel/fax 971 63 90 37
An inexpensive *pension*.
The terrace has breathtaking
views of the valley below.

Read's Hotel
near Santa Maria
tel 971 14 02 62 fax 971 14 07 62
An exclusive hotel with British
elegance in a beautifully
restored old *finca*.

Reserva Rotana
Cami de S'Avall, Manacor
tel 971 84 56 85 fax 971 55 52 58
A superb *finca*, converted into
an elegant hotel with twenty-
two rooms, a private golf
course, and tennis facilities.

Vistamar
Ctra. Valldemossa a Andratx,
Valldemossa
tel 971 63 23 00 fax 971 61 25 83
A grand *finca* in the country,
surrounded by gardens and
with sweeping views of the sea.

Restaurants, cafés, and bars

Abacanto
Cami Nou, Sa Indioleria,
Palma
tel 971 43 06 24
Another late-night bar from
the creators of Abaco (listed
below).

Abaco
c/Sant Joan, Palma
tel 971 71 49 39
Be prepared to look stylish in
this elegantly decadent and
very late-night bar in an old
palace; opera music plays at
full volume and showers of
rose petals flutter down from
the ceiling.

Bens D'Avall
Urbanization Costa de Deià a
Sóller, Sóller
tel 971 63 23 81
Excellent dining on a terrace
that looks out across the sea.

Café d'es Case
Palau Sólleric, Passeig d'es
Born 27, Palma
A chic arts café in a recently
restored and redecorated
building that is also a venue
for art exhibitions.

Café Lirico
Avda. d'Antoni Mauri, Palma
This café is an institution –
a hangout for generations of
Palma's intelligentsia.

Café Parisien
c/Ciutat 18, Artà
tel 971 83 54 40
A stylish continental bar-
restaurant with an attractive
garden.

Can Antuna
Fornalutx
In this restaurant, fine
Majorcan food is served by
Jaime Bosquet and his family.

Can Costa
Ctra. Valldemossa a Deià
km 2.5, Valldemossa
tel 971 61 22 63
Classic Majorcan food is
served in the elegant dining
room. During warmer weather,
the outdoor terrace is pleasant.

Can Toni Moreno
off Ctra. Valldemossa a
Andratx, Porto Es Canonge
This tiny settlement is an
unlikely place for a restaurant,
but the fresh fish is worth the
drive alone. The specialty of

zarzuela with lobster is very
good and well worth a try.

Celler Sa Premsa
Plaça Bisbe Berenguer de
Palou 8, Palma
Good, inexpensive Majorcan
food in a large rustic "cellar."

El Bungalow
Cuidad Jardin, Palma
tel 971 26 27 38
Two miles from Palma, a beach-
front restaurant specializing
in paella and fish. The view of
the city at night is lovely.

El Café
Grand Hotel, Palma
tel 971 72 80 77
An elegant modern restaurant
in this beautifully restored
belle époque building.

El Olivo
Hotel La Residencia, Deià
tel 971 63 90 11
Celebrated cuisine is served in
the former oil pressing room
of the old *finca*, which now
forms the heart of this hotel.

El Pesquero
c/Moll de la Llotja, Palma
tel 971 71 52 20

Local fishermen can still be
seen repairing nets beside this
modern bar-restaurant.

Es Poblet
near Castel d'Alaró, Alaró
Paletilla de cordero (shoulder
of lamb) is slowly roasted
in huge ovens fired by olive
wood. Go armed with a
hearty appetite and rugged
suspension on your car. The
journey up the mountain road
has beautiful views of Palma.
Definitely worth the trip.

Es Vergeret
Cala Tuent, Escorca
Turn off the road before
Torrente de Pareis to reach
this restaurant, which has
a terrace that reaches out
toward the sea. The setting
alone will be enough to
convince you that you have
had the best paella of your life.

Forn des Tèatre
Plaça Weyler 9, Palma
Behind an *art nouveau*
storefront is a *pâtisserie* that
specializes in traditional
Majorcan *ensaimadas*.

Koldo Royo
Paseo Maritimo, Palma
tel 971 73 24 35
Excellent international
cuisine in a romantic setting
overlooking the bay of Palma.

La Boveda
near Plaça de Sa Llonja, Palma
A traditional tapas bar with
an excellent atmosphere.

Parlament
c/Conquistador 11, Palma
tel 971 72 60 26
An old-fashioned restaurant
with typical dishes like "paella
for the blind" – chicken and
rabbit, without bones.

Restaurant Can Jaume
c/Luis Salvador, Deià
Classic Majorcan food served
in unpretentious surroundings.
Sisters Magdalena and Maria
have served generations of
diners here, including King
Juan Carlos. A favorite of
native Majorcans and "local
foreigners" alike.

Restaurant Can Lluc
Cala Deià, Deià
Lucas Morell and his family
serve fresh fish on a terrace
located in one of the most
beautiful coves on Majorca.

Restaurant Pipistrella
c/Conceptió 34, Palma
tel 971 71 56 01
This restaurant has beautiful
vaulted ceilings and striking
paintings. The food prepared
by the Belgian chef-owner has
a distinct Italian influence.

Restaurant Plaça Cort
Plaça Cort 15, Palma
tel 971 71 86 28
This elegant restaurant serves
international cuisine. Designed
by Antonio Obrador, it has a
grand *trompe l'œil* ceiling that
draws its inspiration from the
royal palace.

Restaurant Porto Pi
Avda. Joan Miró 174, Palma
tel 971 40 00 87
Imaginative yet elegant food
is served in this highly
acclaimed restaurant.

IBIZA

Sant Joan

Santa Gertrudis

Sant Antoni

Santa Eulalia

Sant Rafel

EIVISSA (IBIZA TOWN)

FORMENTERA

SANT FRANCESC
XAVIER

Fornells
Cuidadella
Es Mercadal
Ferreries
Alaior
MENORCA
MAHÓN

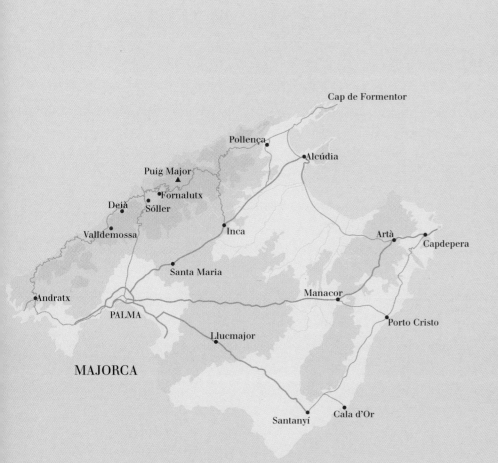

Cap de Formentor
Pollença
Alcúdia
Puig Major
▲
Fornalutx
Deià
Sóller
Valldemossa
Inca
Andratx
Santa Maria
Artà
Capdepera
PALMA
Manacor
Llucmajor
Porto Cristo
MAJORCA
Santanyí
Cala d'Or

THE BALEARIC ISLANDS

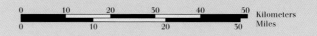

0   10   20   30   40   50 Kilometers
0   10   20   30 Miles

Restaurant Vista Mar
Ctra. Valldemossa a Andratx,
Valldemossa
tel 971 61 23 00
The dining room in this old
finca opens out onto a pretty
terrace. A stroll through the
gardens offers a beautiful view
of Porto Valldemossa far below.

San Sebastian
c/Felipe Bauza, Deià
tel 971 63 94 17
A charming restaurant
that specializes in elegant
continental cuisine.

Sa Teulera
Ctra. Sóller a Lluc, Sóller
tel 971 63 11 11
The house specialty of *lechona*
(roast suckling pig) slowly
turned over a bed of glowing
coals is just one reason to visit
this restaurant.

Ses Porxeres
Ctra. Sóller a Palma, Bunyola
tel 971 63 37 92
Located by the Gardens of
Alfabia, this restaurant serves
traditional Majorcan food.

Son Moragues
Valldemossa
tel 971 61 61 11
Once owned by the Archduke
Luis Salvador, this historic
finca now serves suitably
grand Majorcan cuisine.

Shops

Almacén Gerards Decoration
c/Mosseu Galines 93,
Sant Llorenç
Specializing in furniture and
decorative items, this shop
displays natural mobiles
and bead curtains crafted
by Conchi, whose home is
featured in this book.

Bujosa
c/Bernardo 53, Santa Maria
tel 971 62 00 54
Traditional Majorcan fabrics
have been produced and sold
since the early nineteenth
century by successive
generations of this family.

Casa Rustica
Centre Ciutat, Santa Maria
Classic Majorcan and Spanish
antiques.

Coconut Company
Ctra. Palma a Artà, Manacor
This shop has a selection of
furniture and furnishings in
a variety of exotic styles that
have been imported from the
Philippines, Thailand, India,
and North Africa.

Eclectica
c/Victoria 4, Palma
As its name implies, the
goods available here form
an eclectic collection.

Encantes
c/Puigdorfila, Palma
An interesting mix of objects
that make ideal gifts.

Estil Gothic
Palau Reial 10, Palma
Home furnishings and
decorative objects in classic
Majorcan style can be found
in this shop located in the area
near the cathedral.

Islas
c/Luis Salvador, Deià
Offers clothing and decorative
objects from Bali, plus arts
and crafts by local artists.

Nexus
c/Luis Salvador, Deià
tel 971 63 93 10
Unusual clothes from Latin
America and the Far East.

Nino Tauro
Plaça Sa Llonja 6, Palma
tel 971 72 35 24
This shop has unique *papier-
mâché* sculptures made by
local artisans.

Son Pax
c/Peletera 13, Palma
tel 971 72 14 55
Sells furniture and furnishings
designed by Leif Ljungstrom
and Agneta Cederlund (both
featured in this book) that
have been made by Majorcan
craftsmen in a contemporary
Mediterranean style.

Valldemossa
This famous village on the west
coast is a magnet for tourists –
but do not be deterred. Some
of the better shops have
wonderful examples of the
traditional Majorcan linens,
ceramics, glassware, and
basketware. Here are a few:
*Capamunta, Es Teix, Giravent,
Jose Ripoll, Muza & Co.*

Vidrios de Gordiola
Ctra. Palma a Manacor km 19,
Algaida
Handblown glassware is
available from this family
studio that has been
established since 1719.

Designers

Denario
c/San Felio 17, Palma
tel 971 72 69 87
The design consultancy
of Antonio Obrador, who is
responsible for three of the
homes featured in this book.

Galleries and museums

Galeria Max
Deià
Changing exhibitions that
feature paintings and
sculptures by local artists.

Fundació Pilar i Joan Miró
c/Joan de Sardakis 29, Palma
tel 971 70 14 20
Exhibits work by Miró and
other modern Spanish artists;
visits to Miró's studio can also
be organized.

*Fundación Yannick y Ben
Jakober*
Sa Bassa Blanca, Mal Pas,
Alcúdia
tel 971 54 67 78
Group visits can be arranged
by telephone to view this
private art collection.

Galeria Benasar
Pollença
Exhibitions of work by
contemporary artists.

*Galeria D'Art – Joanna
Kunstmann*
Plaça de Canal 16, Santanyí
Exhibits contemporary art.

La Tafona
Hotel La Residencia, Deià
Exhibitions of work by local
artists. The shows change
every two-to-three weeks.

Palau Sólleric
Passeig d'es Born 27, Palma
Changing exhibits of historic
and contemporary art in this
grand palace.

Sala Pelaires
Pelaires 5, Palma
Exhibitions of work by famous
twentieth-century artists.

S'Estació
Sineu
Exhibitions of contemporary
artists' work are housed in this
old railroad station.

Places of interest

Almudaina
Palma
Known by its Arab name, the
royal palace was established
by the Romans. It was later
developed as a grand palace
by the Moors and is now the
Balearic palace of King Juan
Carlos. The throne rooms and
museums are open for visits.

Arab Baths
c/Can Serra 7, Palma
Vestiges of the Moorish era
can still be found in the heart
of the old city.

Calderes
near Sant Joan
This old *finca* is now a private
museum that also has animals.

Castell de Bellver
northwest of Palma
Situated on a hill overlooking
Palma is the citadel and the
residence of the Majorcan

monarchy during the
fourteenth century.

Coves del Drac
near Porto Cristo
The Dragon Caves are
the largest of several cave
systems that are found on the
island. These caves have an
enormous underground lake.

Gardens of Alfabia
off the Sóller-Palma road near
the mouth of the new tunnel
The Arabian gardens created
by a Moorish nobleman.

La Granja
near Esporles
A restored estate that now
has displays of traditional
farm life and crafts.

La Seu
Palma
This is one of the finest
Gothic cathedrals in Europe.
Its fabulous altar canopy was
designed by Gaudí. Definitely
not to be missed.

Mirador d'es Colomer
Cap de Formentor
Reached by a vertigo-inducing
path, this turret offers an

astounding view across the
Bay of Alcúdia.

Roman Amphitheater
near Alcúdia
Alcúdia was the Roman capital
of Balearis Major. There
are several traces of Roman
buildings in this vicinity,
including this amphitheater.

Sa Cartuja
Valldemossa
This is a fascinating place
to visit. Of particular interest
is a seventeenth-century
monastery that has beautiful
gardens with wonderful views
of the valley below.

Sa Llotja
off the Paseo Maritimo, Palma
This fabulous Gothic building
was the stock exchange of
Palma from the middle of the
fifteenth century. It is also a
venue for major art exhibitions.

Talayot de Ses Paisses
Artà
Remains of a prehistoric
Bronze Age settlement
with perimeter walls that,
amazingly, are still intact.

Torrente de Pareis
Sa Calobra, Escorca
Known as the "Grand Canyon
of Majorca," this gorge is
a mere 100 feet wide; its walls,
however, rise straight up to
2,000 feet. This is an awesome
place that is worth a visit,
at least for the twisting
drive down.

Tren de Sóller
Sóller
An old train that runs through
the countryside from Sóller
to Palma. Another old wooden
open tram line runs from the
center of Sóller to Porto Sóller.

Yacht brokers

*Balearic International
Yachtbrokers*
Club de Mar, Palma
tel 971 40 41 09
Exceptional sailing yachts and
motor yachts for sale or rental.

IBIZA

Hotels

Cas Pla
Sant Miquel de Balanzat
tel 971 33 45 87 fax 971 33 46 04
A charming hotel in the north
of the island.

El Corsario
c/Poniente 5, Eivissa
tel 971 39 32 12 fax 971 39 19 53
Formerly a meeting place
for bohemians in the 1960s
and 1970s, this old townhouse
offers small rooms with a
huge view.

Hacienda Na Xamena
Sant Miquel de Balanzat
tel 971 33 45 00 fax 971 33 45 14
A five-star hotel set in a group
of typical white Ibizan houses.
All furnishings are from La
Maison de l'Elephant.

Hostal Cala Moli
Apartado 105, Sant Josép
tel 971 80 02 02
A quiet, friendly place
surrounded by pine trees.

Hotel Les Terrasses
tel 971 33 26 43 fax 971 33 89 78
Ctra. de Santa Eulalia km 1,
Eivissa
The rooms and suites of this
hotel are set in a collection
of small houses in the
countryside. There are tennis
facilities, a swimming pool,
and wonderful food.

Las Brisas
Porroig
tel 971 80 21 93 fax 971 80 23 28
An exclusive hotel with
Moroccan interiors, two suites,
and six rooms with terraces.

La Ventana
Sa Carrosa 13, Eivissa
tel 971 39 08 57 fax 971 39 01 45
A small, charming hotel in
Dalt Vila (the old upper town
within the walls).

Restaurants, cafés, and bars

Balafi
Ctra. Sant Joan, near
Sant Lorenç
An inexpensive restaurant
that is a favorite with the
locals. The homemade
sausages, ham, and grilled
meats are particularly tasty.

Ca Na Joana
Ctra. Eivissa a Sant Josép km 10
tel 971 80 01 58
Set in a converted old *finca*,
this French/Catalan kitchen
opens for dinner only.

Can Costa
Plaça de la Iglesia, Santa
Gertrudis
tel 971 19 70 21
A tapas bar that overlooks the
church in this lovely hamlet.

Can Den Parra
c/San Rafel 3, Eivissa
tel 971 39 11 14
Catalan food served in a
pretty outdoor setting.

Can Pujol
Badia de Sant Antoni, Port des
Torrent
tel 971 34 14 07
Notable for the freshness of
its ingredients and location
(it has a terrace that overlooks
the sea). The house specialty
is fish with *aïoli*.

Chez Françoise
Plaça del Parque, Eivissa
tel 971 39 19 19
Excellent food on a terrace in
a quiet square.

El Boldado
on the Cala d'Hort near
Sant Josép, turn left onto a
private road (Camino Privat)
at Las Cruces
tel 908 83 88 27 (mobile only)
On the southwest coast, this
restaurant is in a dramatic
setting overlooking Es Vedra.
Fresh fish and paellas are
served with a stunning view
of the sea and the sunset.

Es Xarou (also known as *Chez
Mariano*)
on the road to San Josép in
Cala Virgin near Cala Jondal
A charming restaurant that
serves delicious fresh fish.

La Bodega del Medio
Obispo Torres Mayans, Eivissa
A café-bar with a rough,
unaffected interior located next
to the gate to the old town.

L'Elephant
Plaça de la Iglesia, Sant Rafel
tel 971 19 80 56
An elegant restaurant that
serves excellent food and has
wonderful views of Eivissa.

Montesol
Plaça Vara del Rey, Eivissa
The terrace of this colonial-
style hotel is an institution;
it has been a meeting place for
morning coffee or afternoon
aperitifs since the 1960s.

Sa Cova
Plaça Santa Lucia, Eivissa
tel 971 19 16 48
A restaurant with a cavelike
interior and a naturally
protected outdoor space.
The food is fresh and tasty.

Tagomago
island off Cala Sant Vicent
A day trip by boat can be
combined with dinner by
eating the day's catch in a
terrace restaurant by the sea.

Victoria
c/de la Cruz, Eivissa
A down-to-earth family
restaurant with fine food.

Shops

A Media Luz
Obispo Torres Mayans 2,
Eivissa
Sells an interesting mixture of
antiques and new items.

Ganesha
c/Montgris 14, Eivissa
A bazaarlike shop that sells
both secondhand clothes and
a selection of antiques.

Herbolaria
c/de la Cruz 23, Eivissa
An old-fashioned herbalist
where "miracle" mixtures are
blended as you watch.

José Pascaal
c/de la Cruz 30, Eivissa
A multitude of baskets and
hammocks produce the
wonderful aroma of natural
materials in this shop.
Traditional products from
Ibiza are also sold.

La Maison de l'Elephant
Ctra. Eivissa a Sant
Antoni, km 2.2
tel 971 31 12 54
Recently launched by interior
designer Bruno Reymond,
this shop sells various items
for the house. The style is
multicultural, with furniture
and household objects that
originate far from Ibiza.

Leather shop
corner of c/Conde de Rosellon
and c/d'Anniball, Eivissa
A workshop/shop that
produces and sells exclusive
handbags and belts.

Pan con Tomate
c/Montgris 2, Eivissa
tel 971 31 12 53
The eclectic shop owned
by interior designer Victor
Esposito – whose apartment
is featured in this book.
The items available range
from heavy country cupboards
to featherlight scarves.

Markets

Las Dalias
close to San Carlos on the
road from Santa Eulalia
A Saturday "hippie market" to
take you back to the 1960s.

Places of interest

Cathedral & Bishop's Palace
Dalt Vila, Eivissa
Built on the site of a Roman
temple and an Arab mosque,
the cathedral dates from the
thirteenth century.

*Museu Arqueológic d'Eivissa i
Formentera*
Dalt Vila, Eivissa
The museum boasts an
extensive collection of
artifacts that date as far back
as the Bronze Age.

Museu d'Art Contemporani
Dalt Vila, Eivissa
The museum has both
changing exhibitions and
a permanent collection by
Spanish and foreign artists.

Santa Gertrudis
This village has a selection of
antique and craft shops. There
are also decent cafés to have
some tapas and a drink while
reflecting on your purchases.

MENORCA

Hotels

Hostal Biniali
Sant Lluís
tel 971 15 17 24 fax 971 15 03 52
Old manor house set within
the countryside.

Hotel Port-Mahón
Avda. Fort de L'Eau 13, Mahón
tel 971 36 26 00 fax 971 35 10 50
A four-star hotel in an English-
style Georgian building with a
magnificent view of the harbor.

La Tortuga
near Alaior
tel/fax 971 37 24 81
Karel Fonteyne has created
a colorful guesthouse that
is featured in this book. The
breakfasts are simple but good,
and the dinners, rich and spicy.

Restaurants

Café Balear
c/Marina, Ciudadella
tel 971 38 00 05
One of the better fish
restaurants in the busy marina.

Ca'n Nito
Moll de Llevant, Mahón
tel 971 36 52 26
A delightful restaurant
overlooking the harbor.

El Horno
c/d'es Forn 12, Ciudadella
tel 971 38 07 67
A pretty bistro.

Es Cap Roig
Cala Mesquida, near Mahón
tel 971 36 37 15
A splendid view by the
sea. The local specialty
of *calderata de llagosta*
(lobster stew) is delicious.

Mar y Vent
Moll de Llevant, Mahón
tel 971 36 90 67
Fish and seafood is served on
the terraces by the harbor.

Plaça d'es Born
Ciudadella
A beautiful old square with
café terraces – it is especially
pretty in the late afternoon.

Restaurante Na Macaret
c/La Punta 33, Es Mercadel
tel 971 37 53 91
Not easy to find but really
worth the effort. The dishes
are unusual and very tasty.

Markets

Plaça de la Libertat,
Ciudadella
A lively, colorful market
reminiscent of the *souks*
of North Africa.

Places of interest

Bibibeguer Vell
A reconstruction of a Moorish fishing village.

Fornells
An especially pretty, naturally protected harbor on the north coast. Two particularly good restaurants are:
Can Miquel
tel 971 37 54 59
Siban's
tel 971 37 66 19
Both serve fresh fish and local specialty dishes.

Taulas de Trepucó
near Mahón
Largest group of prehistoric *talayots* (rocky mounds) on the island; also the site of fortifications built in 1756 by the Duc de Richelieu.

Torre d'en Gaumes
The site of a remarkably well-preserved prehistoric settlement that was inhabited until medieval times.

Troglodyte dwellings
Cala Morell
Some of the most important Bronze Age caves in Europe.

FORMENTERA

Hotels

Capri
Playa es Pujols
tel 971 32 83 52
A pleasant, inexpensive hotel and restaurant.

Hostal Fonda Pepe
San Fernando
tel 971 32 80 33
Bob Dylan reputedly stayed in this charming hotel in the 1960s. It is ideal for those nostalgic for the hippie era.

Restaurants and cafés

Can Gaviny
between Sant Francesc and San Ferran
A trendy, colorful restaurant.

Es Cap
Ctra. Cap Berbería
tel 971 32 21 04
Friendly service in a restaurant that specializes in fish and grilled meat.

Fonda Rafalet
Es Caló
tel 971 13 65 92
A hotel by the sea with a fine view of the coastline.

Plate
Plaça de Constitucion, c/Jaime Primér, Sant Francesc
A lively café terrace next to the hippie market held every morning except Sunday.

Sa Cava
near Punta Pedra
Ideal for dining while admiring the sunset over the rocky landscape.

Shops

Casa Blanca
c/d'Isidro, Macabich
Sells interior items.

El Abanico
c/Jaime Primér, Sant Francesc
Offers a combination of antiques, local ceramics, and Mediterranean crafts.

Places of interest

Cap Berbería
One of the earliest settlements on the islands, dating from the Neolithic and Bronze ages.

Sa Tanca Vella
Sant Francesc
A tiny fourteenth-century chapel constructed for the first wave of settlers from Ibiza.

The authors wish to offer thanks to all those who have welcomed them into their homes and shared their enchantment with these islands; and they are grateful for the extra time the owners have taken to discuss the details of their homes.

Lanning Aldrich: I wish to thank all the subjects of this book for their ready and gracious cooperation. I would also like to thank Georges and Cecilie Sheridan, talented and dedicated artists both, for their comments and support, especially with respect to the arts community in Deià and Majorca; Jeff and Margaret Flood, who helped immensely, particularly in clarifying matters of linguistics (in the Balearics, the delineations between Castilian, Catalan, Mallorquí, Eivissenc, and Menorquí are never quite as straightforward as the rules would seem to indicate); and Emma-Louise O'Reilly, who has been dedicated and diligent in shaping the text. Finally, words like "style," "flair," and "taste" are used frequently in this book, and these are some terms that very much help to describe my wife, Shelley Page, who shares my love of these islands and has been steadfast in her comments, criticisms, and advice.

Commissioning editor: Suzannah Gough
Managing editor: Richard Atkinson
Editorial assistant: Tanya Robinson

Art director: Leslie Harrington
Art editor: Karen Bowen
Map illustration: Tony Seddon

Production: Amanda Sneddon

Published in 1998 and distributed in the U.S. by
Stewart, Tabori & Chang,
a division of U.S. Media Holdings, Inc.
115 West 18th Street, New York, NY 10011

Photographs © Sølvi dos Santos 1998
Text © Lanning Aldrich 1998
Design and layout © Conran Octopus Limited 1998

Library of Congress Catalog Card Number: 98-86005

ISBN: 1-55670-847-5

Printed in China

10 9 8 7 6 5 4 3 2 1